MW00587305

The Courage
to See

The Courage to See

DAILY INSPIRATION FROM GREAT LITERATURE

Greg Garrett *and* Sabrina Fountain

WJK WESTMINSTER
JOHN KNOX PRESS
LOUISVILLE • KENTUCKY

First edition
Published by Westminster John Knox Press
Louisville, Kentucky

19 20 21 22 23 24 25 26 27 28—10 9 8 7 6 5 4 3 2 1

Unless otherwise indicated, Scripture quotations are from the New Revised Standard Version of the Bible, copyright © 1989 by the Division of Christian Education of the National Council of the Churches of Christ in the U.S.A., and are used by permission.

Book design by Drew Stevens and Allison Taylor
Cover design by Barbara LeVan Fisher, www.levanfisherdesign.com

Library of Congress Cataloging-in-Publication Data

Names: Garrett, Greg, author.
Title: The courage to see : daily inspiration from great literature / Greg
    Garrett and Sabrina Fountain.
Description: First edition. | Louisville, Kentucky : Westminster John Knox
    Press, 2019. | Includes bibliographical references and index. | Summary:
    Book lovers know there is something sacred in the stories, poetry, and
    insight of even the most secular books. This 365-day devotional
    celebrates the beauty of literature and its ability to illuminate
    elements of the Divine, present all around us. Pairing excerpts from
    more than two-hundred literary works with thought-provoking scriptures
    and brief prayers, this spiritual guide invites readers to draw closer
    to God through the words of both classic and modern authors.
Identifiers: LCCN 2019005258 (print) | ISBN 9780664263089 (hbk. : alk.
    paper)
Subjects: LCSH: Devotional literature. | Bible--Quotations. | Religion in
    literature. | Quotations, English.
Classification: LCC BV4832.3 .G37 2019 (print) | LCC BV4832.3 (ebook) |
    DDC 242/.2--dc23
LC record available at https://lccn.loc.gov/2019005258
LC ebook record available at https://lccn.loc.gov/2019980521

PRINTED IN THE UNITED STATES OF AMERICA

♾ The paper used in this publication meets the minimum requirements of
the American National Standard for Information Sciences—
Permanence of Paper for Printed Library Materials, ANSI Z39.48-1992.

Most Westminster John Knox Press books are available at special quantity discounts when purchased in bulk by corporations, organizations, and special-interest groups. For more information, please e-mail SpecialSales@wjkbooks.com.

Contents

It has seemed to me sometimes as though the Lord breathes on this poor gray ember of Creation and it turns to radiance—for a moment or a year or the span of a life. And then it sinks back into itself again, and to look at it no one would know it had anything to do with fire, or light. . . . Wherever you turn your eyes the world can shine like transfiguration. You don't have to bring a thing to it except a little willingness to see. Only, who could have the courage to see it?

MARILYNNE ROBINSON, GILEAD

Foreword

When I was a child, I wanted to sleep with my books, something my mom wouldn't allow because I slept on the top bunk, and she didn't want them falling down and hitting my sister. I wanted to sleep with them not to secretly read them under the covers with a flashlight, but to have them near me, to curl up with them, like stuffed animals. Of course I loved the stories, the characters, the imaginary worlds, but I also loved the books as objects. The colors and patterns of the covers, the texture of the paper, the feel of the pages when I strummed them out with my thumb. I was scrupulous with my books, never leaving them splayed open to keep my place, never folding down corners, and absolutely never writing in them. *Very* rarely, if a book was particularly dear to me, I would put in one of the *Ex Libris* bookplates I got for my birthday one year. This still felt like some sort of transgression, as if I was occupying a space that didn't really belong to me, but which welcomed me nonetheless.

If I am honest, not much has changed. I still have a deep sense of reverence about books and still find them profoundly comforting as physical objects. I feel better when I am surrounded by them, whether shelves and shelves at bookstores, piles on the bedside table, or endless aisles at the library. In this I am surely typical of most English majors, for whom book love comes early and stays forever. And English majors or not, readers' book love is alive and well, despite the advent of e-books and audio books and online publishing. The resistance to letting go of the book as object has been fierce and relatively successful. Many of us still want our stories to be physical.

Of course I also loved the contents of my books. Like any bookish child, I was always having to be torn away from reading to come to the dinner table, to get out the door; I just wanted to keep finding out what happened. I loved the unfolding of the characters, the buildup of the plot, the final telling of the end. I liked most endings—certainly the happy ones, sometimes the sad ones even more—and to this day I have a very particular feeling whenever I finish a book. When I was about ten, I remember finishing the last page of Madeleine L'Engle's *A Wind in the Door* while I was taking a bath. I closed the book with a feeling I had never known before, an amalgam of chill, wonder, and mystery. I felt as though what had just happened to me was something beyond what I could put into words, yet somehow deeply resonant. I felt at the same time a profound *Yes* and a bewildering *What in the world was that?* I closed the book and held it pressed against my forehead for a while.

When I think about this relationship between object and contents, tangibility and story, I think about my interaction with Scripture. My relationship with God's story told in Scripture frequently changes shape. At times I can enter it with joy, and it feels vibrant, beautiful, and alive. Other times I find it baffling, difficult, hard to face. Or I *want* to want to engage the story but am tired or discouraged, stretched thin by deadlines and caring for kids and doing what needs to be done. In these harder times, it helps me to go to objects, to forms, to be OK with not thinking about content and instead allowing the container to be a means of grace. Hearing the Scripture read, but not trying to analyze it. Sitting with my love over a beautiful meal. Letting the prayers of a friend be enough when I don't have any of my own. All of these things carry me along.

So too, in a way, reading books, whether "classic" or contemporary, fiction or nonfiction, can be a means of grace. It can be the *story in front of the story*—writing that pulls us into the Big Story, that allows us to come there by meeting us in the specificity of our human lives. The passages selected for this book range widely—writers from centuries ago, writers still alive today, men and women from countries around the globe—but they all shimmer with humanity, with our questions and affections and injustices and wonder.

In likening these works to *stories in front of the story*, I should clarify that I don't see them as simple conduits, or as stepping-stones, useful to help us get somewhere else. The fundamental Christian belief that human beings are made in the image of God casts a sheen over what we make, what we do, how we love, what we hope. These books and these passages, in themselves, show us what it is to be what we are. They make us realize our lives, take notice. Books can make us wrestle, find peace, get angry, feel consoled. We can see ourselves, catch glimpses of who we want to be, who we don't want to be. In many ways, books, stories, and words are about paying attention.

What a number of the passages selected here pay attention to is mystery. It might be that I have gravitated toward these because of the phase of life I find myself in, approaching "middle age," with my children just getting old enough that I have some space in my mind and heart and body to take notice. And what I notice is how bewildering everything is—in ways both marvelous and terrifying—and how in the face of that bewildering, what I want more of, every day, is gratitude. All the stories are so much bigger and more meaningful than I realized, and I want to pay attention to them. I want to be a witness.

In *A Tale of Two Cities*, Charles Dickens describes a "wonderful fact to reflect upon, that every human creature is constituted to be that profound secret and mystery to every other." I would go even farther than this, to say that quite often each of us is a mystery and secret even to ourselves. Books can reveal us to ourselves, in ways that are surprising, unsettling, or completely apropos for our particular space and moment. They can give us that feeling I had as a ten-year-old, where something true about the world is uncovered, where something of our true identity is reflected back to us. Books can make us attentive to our lives and, therefore, attentive to the places in which God is meeting us. It is in this one simple, astonishing life that there is the possibility of God meeting us. And, as incarnational theology attests, meet us God did. God's story, God's self, made physical.

A favorite painting of mine is *Ida Reading a Letter*, by Danish artist Vilhelm Hammershøi. Like nearly all of Hammershøi's paintings, *Ida Reading a Letter* feels subdued, cool, and sparse: in a nearly monochrome room, a woman stands in profile next to a table and looks down at the letter in her hands. The ebony of her dress and her dusky hair pulled back in a bun are a dark anchor on the canvas. The curve of her body, the tilt of her head, serve as soft counterpoints to the stark geometry of the doors, the table, the molding around the room. The reader is a common subject in paintings: one individual quietly absorbed in the world of a book or a letter, seemingly oblivious to his or her surroundings. To me these reading paintings always feel like images of the unseen in the midst of the seen, a strange witnessing of someone who is in the act of witnessing something else. What world do the readers occupy? Where is the story leading them, and what reality is taking shape in their imaginations? *Ida Reading a Letter* is a deceptively simple painting—it seems quiet and quotidian, with its coffeepot and dishes, the minimalism of the interior, the firm serenity of the woman—but the more you look at it the more you see going on. One closed door and one open door, their strong verticals tethering the painting. One woman, by herself, but not lonely. It is a painting of the plain, physical, everyday world. A world that is stunningly beautiful.

When I look at a Hammershøi painting, so silent yet so eloquent, I am drawn into that experience of the world. Drawn into the vision of someone who reminds us that the everyday is replete with meaning, if only we will pay attention to it. Great art, whether visual, musical, written, or otherwise, ushers us toward this kind of attention. The Marilynne Robinson quote from which the title of this book comes reminds us: "Wherever you turn your eyes the world can shine like transfiguration. You don't have to bring a thing to it except a little willingness to see. Only, who could have the courage to see it?"

This is the experience of living a life, realities that will "shine like transfiguration," yet which can so easily slip by unnoticed. My children, caught up in wonder in the woods. Seeds we planted in the garden, miraculously sprouting out of their darkness. Words written by someone I will never meet, but which still somehow speak directly to the specificity of my right-now life.

Sometimes I wonder why it is that seeing these things takes courage. Perhaps because seeing might ask us to change, which is hard, or, even harder, seeing might implicate us somehow, bring to light something we would rather not face. Maybe seeing will make us newer, wiser, more deeply rooted people than we thought was possible, and there is a special kind of fear for what we long for but are afraid will elude us. Life is potential. Life is disappointment. In both cases, life is more than we thought, more holy and hard and full of meaning than we anticipated. And we are asked to be witnesses of that. Of all of that. As we read the words of the authors included here, it is my belief that they attest to what the authors have seen and that they serve as an invitation to us as readers to be courageous enough to see along with them.

The beloved books of my childhood are having a second run in my life, now that I have my own young children. Reading to my twins, I find myself wondering what it must be like to encounter the stories for the first time, the slate so amazingly clean, the ending unknown. Happily, I find that my own reaction to these books hasn't diminished, however distanced I am now from my very first encounter with them. I am still enchanted by the candy world of *Charlie and the Chocolate Factory* (every child's dream!), I still cry when Aslan dies in *The Lion, the Witch, and the Wardrobe*, and I laugh even more at the quirky humor of the *Frog and Toad* stories. Some books from my adult life have the same power as childhood ones; I will always get angry that Laurie marries Amy in *Little Women*, my heart will always race in the nefarious unfolding of *Crime and Punishment*, I will always have to stop reading and pause after so many arresting lines in *Love in the Time of Cholera*.

Whether we are reading a work for the first time or the fifth, books shape who we are and how we think. In childhood, books somehow create our stories along with us, molding our expectations and affections, giving us a sense of the arc of a story or of a life. When we are older, that shaping is different, colored by recognition as well as epiphany. We come to stories with more of a past, more opportunities to see our lives reflected. As George Eliot writes in *The Mill on the Floss,* "Childhood has no forebodings; but then, it is soothed by no memories of outlived sorrow." When we are older, everything is not new, but everything is infused with memory. In adulthood we come to books as, to adjust D. H. Lawrence's phrase, "people who have come through."

In Romans 4:17, a verse I have always loved for both the enigmatic poetry and the promise of it, the apostle Paul describes God's promise to Abraham. Abraham, Paul says, ultimately did not despair over his by-all-accounts-hopeless chances of having a child with his wife Sarah (though it has to be said that his faith was often quite circumspect, which should serve as encouragement to us all). Instead of giving up all hope of a child, Abraham chose to have faith "in the presence of the God in whom he believed, who gives life to the dead and calls into existence the things that do not exist." The version I learned growing up says that God "calls the things that are not, as though they were" (Rom. 4:17b, World English Bible). I love the closely juxtaposed contradiction in the language, the fairy-tale, magic quality of it. It's not that something metamorphoses, from not being to being. Instead, it simply does not exist, but God says, *It does.* God's calling, God's naming of things, effects both the renewal and the promise.

This is profound and radical seeing, taking all of our courage to embrace. In this verse, God's naming is so far from our way of seeing things and goes against our settled-on version of how things are. The Bible is full of these transformations, new life that starts off in the most dubious and hopeless of situations. And these transformations are always rooted in the ordinary, simple, very physical reality of the world. An old man and old woman as the parents of a new and chosen people. A lowly shepherd as the king of that people. A young, unmarried girl as the one to carry the Savior. That Savior: a poor, vulnerable, common-yet-miraculous infant.

All of us as readers will come to these passages from literature and Scripture differently. We will bring to them the specificity of our experiences, our histories, our longings. We will come to them with youth or age, with varying degrees of health in our bodies, with our own places of deep joy and expectation, of sorrow and quiet shame. Most likely we will recognize ourselves in many of the passages, and even more likely, that recognition will change depending on the day, the year, the ways that life and time have changed our sight. That continual renewal of words—the ways in which something that slipped right past me when I read it before will all of a sudden stop me in my tracks—that is one of the moments of transfiguration I see. The transfiguring possibility and potential of language—Word and words—spoken, received, witnessed, and shared. *"And the Word became flesh and lived among us."*

Sabrina Fountain
December 2018
Waco, Texas

1

Isn't it queer: there are only two or three human stories, and they go on repeating themselves as fiercely as if they had never happened before; like the larks in this country, that have been singing the same five notes over for thousands of years.

O PIONEERS! BY WILLA CATHER, 1913

What has been is what will be,
    and what has been done is what will be done;
    there is nothing new under the sun.

ECCLESIASTES 1:9

Holy One, help us to hear the stories of your children afresh, to grow in wisdom and compassion as we continue to sing of your love and mercy.

2

As a Scot and a Presbyterian, my father believed that man by nature was a mess and had fallen from an original state of grace. Somehow, I early developed the notion that he had done this by falling from a tree. As for my father, I never knew whether he believed God was a mathematician but he certainly believed God could count and that only by picking up God's rhythms were we able to regain power and beauty. Unlike many Presbyterians, he often used the word "beautiful."

A RIVER RUNS THROUGH IT AND OTHER STORIES
BY NORMAN MACLEAN, 1976

I consider that the sufferings of this present time are not worth comparing with the glory about to be revealed to us. For the creation waits with eager longing for the revealing of the children of God; for the creation was subjected to futility, not of its own will but by the will of the one who subjected it, in hope that the creation itself will be set free from its bondage to decay and will obtain the freedom of the glory of the children of God. We know that the whole creation has been groaning in labor pains until now; and not only the creation, but we ourselves, who have the first fruits of the Spirit, groan inwardly while we wait for adoption, the redemption of our bodies.

ROMANS 8:18–23

Holy God, instruct us in the rhythms that will set all creation free from bondage so that strength and beauty may be born within us.

3

I did not care what it was all about. All I wanted to know was how to live in it. Maybe if you found out how to live in it you learned from that what it was all about.

THE SUN ALSO RISES BY ERNEST HEMINGWAY, 1926

I will meditate on your precepts,
    and fix my eyes on your ways.
I will delight in your statutes;
    I will not forget your word.

PSALM 119:15–16

Teach us, Lord, what matters in life, and how to live it so that we may live in you, now and always.

4

M y eyes already touch the sunny hill,
  going far ahead of the road I have begun.
So we are grasped by what we cannot grasp;
it has inner light, even from a distance—

and changes us, even if we do not reach it,
into something else, which, hardly sensing it,
we already are; a gesture waves us on
answering our own wave . . .
but what we feel is the wind in our faces.

"A WALK" BY RAINER MARIA RILKE, 1924

O LORD, my heart is not lifted up,
   my eyes are not raised too high;
I do not occupy myself with things
   too great and too marvelous for me.
But I have calmed and quieted my soul,
   like a weaned child with its mother.

PSALM 131:1-2

Holy One, may our souls, minds, and bodies find their rest with you, especially in the face of things we can't understand.

5

L ove can't be pinned down by a definition, and it certainly can't be proved, any more than anything else important in life can be proved. Love is people, is a person.

CIRCLE OF QUIET BY MADELEINE L'ENGLE, 1972

In this is love, not that we loved God but that he loved us and sent his Son to be the atoning sacrifice for our sins. Beloved, since God loved us so much, we also ought to love one another.

1 JOHN 4:10–11

Lord Christ, may your life capture us, that we might be filled with love that gives itself to others.

6

Why not let the pears cling
    to the empty branch?
All your coaxing will only make
a bitter fruit—
let them cling, ripen of themselves,
test their own worth,
nipped, shriveled by the frost,
to fall at last but fair
with a russet coat.

FROM "SHELTERED GARDEN" BY H.D., 1916

It is vain that you rise up early
    and go late to rest,
eating the bread of anxious toil;
    for he gives sleep to his beloved.

PSALM 127:2

*Maker of all things, forgive us for thinking that we can work
harder, do more, make ourselves more of what we want to be.
Grant us the peace that comes from entrusting ourselves to you.*

7

If the concept of God has any validity or any use, it can only be to make us larger, freer, and more loving. If God cannot do this, then it is time we got rid of Him.

THE FIRE NEXT TIME BY JAMES BALDWIN, 1963

Every generous act of giving, with every perfect gift, is from above, coming down from the Father of lights, with whom there is no variation or shadow due to change. In fulfillment of his own purpose he gave us birth by the word of truth, so that we would become a kind of first fruits of his creatures.

JAMES 1:17-18

God of every good and perfect gift, give us the strength to manifest your love and compassion in the world today.

8

This you may say of man—when theories change and crash, when schools, philosophies, when narrow dark alleys of thought, national, religious, economic, grow and disintegrate, man reaches, stumbles forward, painfully, mistakenly sometimes. Having stepped forward, he may slip back, but only half a step, never the full step back.

THE GRAPES OF WRATH BY JOHN STEINBECK, 1939

If I go forward, he is not there;
    or backward, I cannot perceive him;
on the left he hides, and I cannot behold him;
    I turn to the right, but I cannot see him.
But he knows the way that I take;
    when he has tested me, I shall come out like gold.

JOB 23:8-10

Holy One, grant that we may arrive at the finish line secure in love, anchored in hope, and firm in our faith in you.

9

She is holding out her flaming heart to God, or shall we say "handing" it to him, exactly as a cook might hand up a corkscrew through the skylight of her basement kitchen to someone who has called down for it from the ground-floor window.

SWANN'S WAY BY MARCEL PROUST, 1913

Through him, then, let us continually offer a sacrifice of praise to God, that is, the fruit of lips that confess his name.

HEBREWS 13:15

Holy Father, we thank you that you receive our humble offerings of praise, however small, with generous and abundant love.

10

It has seemed to me sometimes as though the Lord breathes on this poor gray ember of Creation and it turns to radiance—for a moment or a year or the span of a life. And then it sinks back into itself again, and to look at it no one would know it had anything to do with fire, or light. . . . Wherever you turn your eyes the world can shine like transfiguration. You don't have to bring a thing to it except a little willingness to see. Only, who could have the courage to see it?

GILEAD BY MARILYNNE ROBINSON, 2004

The heavens are telling the glory of God;
    and the firmament proclaims his handiwork.
Day to day pours forth speech,
    and night to night declares knowledge.

PSALM 19:1–2

Source of all beauty, help us to have the courage to see this Creation illuminated by your glory and goodness, and to know that we are an essential part of it.

11

I call them friends, though a week ago we none of us knew there were such folks in the world. But being anxious and sorrowful about the same things makes people friends quicker than anything, I think.

MARY BARTON BY ELIZABETH GASKELL, 1848

I was overjoyed when some of the friends arrived and testified to your faithfulness to the truth, namely how you walk in the truth. . . . Beloved, you do faithfully whatever you do for the friends, even though they are strangers to you.

3 JOHN 3, 5

Friendship is a precious gift, O Lord. Help us know its value and love those who offer it.

12

Jo did not recognize her good angels at once, because they wore familiar shapes, and used the simple spells best fitted to poor humanity. . . . Her mother came to comfort her, not with words only, but the patient tenderness that soothes by a touch, tears that were mute reminders of a greater grief than Jo's, and broken whispers, more eloquent than prayers, because hopeful resignation went hand in hand with natural sorrow.

LITTLE WOMEN BY LOUISA MAY ALCOTT, 1869

He heals the brokenhearted,
  and binds up their wounds.

PSALM 147:3

Our Father, when we are broken and filled with sorrow, may we know in the deep places of our hearts that you are the God who suffers with us.

13

That's why I like listening to Schubert while I'm driving. Like I said, it's because all his performances are imperfect. A dense, artistic kind of imperfection stimulates your consciousness, keeps you alert. If I listen to some utterly perfect performance of an utterly perfect piece while I'm driving, I might want to close my eyes and die right then and there. But listening to the D major, I can feel the limits of what humans are capable of—that a certain type of perfection can only be realized through a limitless accumulation of the imperfect. And personally I find that encouraging.

KAFKA ON THE SHORE BY HARUKI MURAKAMI, 2002

For who sees anything different in you? What do you have that you did not receive? And if you received it, why do you boast as if it were not a gift?

1 CORINTHIANS 4:7

Loving Father, what place is there for perfectionism, when all that we have and all that we are is simply and miraculously a gift from you? Teach us to embrace our limits, to find peace in being who you made us to be.

14

This strangely novel situation of opening his trouble to his Raveloe neighbours, of sitting in the warmth of a hearth not his own, and feeling the presence of faces and voices which were his nearest promise of help, had doubtless its influence on Marner, in spite of his passionate preoccupation with his loss. Our consciousness rarely registers the beginning of a growth within us any more than without us: there have been many circulations of the sap before we detect the smallest sign of the bud.

SILAS MARNER BY GEORGE ELIOT, 1861

He also said, "The kingdom of God is as if someone would scatter seed on the ground, and would sleep and rise night and day, and the seed would sprout and grow, he does not know how."

MARK 4:26-27

Lord, thank you for the hope and promise of newness, which comes to life in ways we do not know!

15

Batter my heart, three-person'd God, for you
As yet but knock, breathe, shine, and seek to mend;
That I may rise and stand, o'erthrow me, and bend
Your force to break, blow, burn, and make me new.

FROM HOLY SONNET XIV BY JOHN DONNE, 1633

My brothers and sisters, whenever you face trials of any
kind, consider it nothing but joy, because you know that
the testing of your faith produces endurance; and let
endurance have its full effect, so that you may be mature
and complete, lacking in nothing.

JAMES 1:2-4

*Break my heart, O God, free me from my own selfishness, and
make me new that I may know you, love you, and serve you
perfectly.*

16

You can't stay in the dark for too long. Something inside you starts to fade, and you become like a starving person, crazy-hungry for light.

THE JOY LUCK CLUB BY AMY TAN, 1989

By the tender mercy of our God,
   the dawn from on high will break upon us,
to give light to those who sit in darkness and in the
     shadow of death,
   to guide our feet into the way of peace.

LUKE 1:78–79

Light of the World, shine on us, and help us reflect your love and light in our own lives.

17

"Nothing is more deceitful," said Darcy, "than the appearance of humility. It is often only carelessness of opinion, and sometimes an indirect boast."

PRIDE AND PREJUDICE BY JANE AUSTEN, 1813

Whoever becomes humble like this child is the greatest in the kingdom of heaven.

MATTHEW 18:4

Lord Christ, may we be more concerned about true humility than the appearance of it.

18

How often the priest had heard the same confession—Man was so limited: he hadn't even the ingenuity to invent a new vice: the animals knew as much. It was for this world that Christ had died: the more evil you saw and heard about you, the greater glory lay around the death; it was too easy to die for what was good or beautiful, for home or children or a civilization—it needed a God to die for the half-hearted and the corrupt.

THE POWER AND THE GLORY BY GRAHAM GREENE, 1940

Indeed, rarely will anyone die for a righteous person—though perhaps for a good person someone might actually dare to die. But God proves his love for us in that while we still were sinners Christ died for us.

ROMANS 5:7–8

Christ our Redeemer, we praise you for your resurrection life, brought to meet us in the midst of our sin, weakness, and rebellion.

19

Why can't reason give greater answers? Why can we throw a question further than we can pull in an answer? Why such a vast net if there's so little fish to catch?

LIFE OF PI BY YANN MARTEL, 2001

Is there anyone among you who, if your child asks for bread, will give a stone? Or if the child asks for a fish, will give a snake? If you then, who are evil, know how to give good gifts to your children, how much more will your Father in heaven give good things to those who ask him!

MATTHEW 7:9–11

Holy One of Abundance, help us to live sure of your love and care for us.

G ive every man thy ear but few thy voice.
Take each man's censure but reserve thy judgment.

HAMLET BY WILLIAM SHAKESPEARE, 1609

A soft answer turns away wrath,
  but a harsh word stirs up anger.
. . . .
A fool despises a parent's instruction,
  but the one who heeds admonition is prudent.

PROVERBS 15:1, 5

Great Source of all knowledge, help us to know what is right and to act with true wisdom.

21

"**D**o not pity the dead, Harry. Pity the living, and, above all those who live without love."

*HARRY POTTER AND THE DEATHLY
HALLOWS* BY J. K. ROWLING, 2007

Therefore be imitators of God, as beloved children, and live in love, as Christ loved us and gave himself up for us, a fragrant offering and sacrifice to God.

EPHESIANS 5:1–2

God, we pray for all those who live without love—and for ourselves, lest we forget that love is our highest calling.

22

When I get honest, I admit I am a bundle of paradoxes. I believe and I doubt, I hope and get discouraged, I love and I hate, I feel bad about feeling good, I feel guilty about not feeling guilty. I am trusting and suspicious. I am honest and I still play games. Aristotle said I am a rational animal; I say I am an angel with an incredible capacity for beer.

To live by grace means to acknowledge my whole life story, the light side and the dark. In admitting my shadow side I learn who I am and what God's grace means.

THE RAGAMUFFIN GOSPEL BY BRENNAN MANNING, 1990

What are human beings that you are mindful of them,
    mortals that you care for them?

Yet you have made them a little lower than God,
    and crowned them with glory and honor.

PSALM 8:4-5

Creator God, we are most marvelously made, and we give thanks that paradoxical as we are, you know us and love us and offer us abundant grace.

23

There is no greater agony than bearing an untold story inside you.

I KNOW WHY THE CAGED BIRD SINGS
BY MAYA ANGELOU, 1969

Do not fear, for I am with you,
  do not be afraid, for I am your God;
I will strengthen you, I will help you,
  I will uphold you with my victorious right hand.

Yes, all who are incensed against you
  shall be ashamed and disgraced;
those who strive against you
  shall be as nothing and shall perish.

ISAIAH 41:10-11

God, give us the strength to bear our stories, and the courage to tell them, secure in your love and acceptance.

24

I don't believe that grief passes away. It has its time and place forever. More time is added to it; it becomes a story within a story. But grief and griever alike endure.

JAYBER CROW BY WENDELL BERRY, 2000

He was despised and rejected by others;
    a man of suffering and acquainted with infirmity;
and as one from whom others hide their faces
    he was despised, and we held him of no account.

Surely he has borne our infirmities
    and carried our diseases;
yet we accounted him stricken,
    struck down by God, and afflicted.

ISAIAH 53:3–4

Lord Jesus, who bore our infirmities and suffered on our account, help us to hold our grief and know your peace.

25

That is the Gospel, this meeting of darkness and light and the final victory of light. That is the fairy tale of the Gospel with, of course, the one crucial difference from all other fairy tales, which is that the claim made for it is that it is true, that it not only happened once upon a time but has kept on happening ever since and is happening still. To preach the Gospel in its original power and mystery is to claim in whatever way the preacher finds it possible to claim it that once upon a time is this time, now.

TELLING THE TRUTH: THE GOSPEL AS TRAGEDY, COMEDY, AND FAIRY TALE BY FREDERICK BUECHNER, 1977

He will swallow up death forever.
Then the Lord GOD will wipe away the tears from all faces,
    and the disgrace of his people he will take away from all
      the earth,
    for the LORD has spoken.

ISAIAH 25:7B–8

Holy Father, whose heart toward us is love, we praise you for the power and mystery of your Great Story of salvation, healing, and resurrection.

26

I never found the companion that was so companionable as solitude.

WALDEN BY HENRY DAVID THOREAU, 1854

But the LORD is in his holy temple;
  let all the earth keep silence before him!

HABAKKUK 2:20

God of the roaring waterfall and of the silent night, help us to listen for you, to know you, and to do your will.

27

Your will includes and is the lord of mine;
   Life to my thoughts within your heart is given;
   My words begin to breathe upon your breath:
Like to the moon am I, that cannot shine
   Alone; for lo! our eyes see nought in heaven
   Save what the living sun illumineth.

FROM SONNET XXX, "LOVE THE LIGHT-GIVER,"
BY MICHELANGELO BUONARROTI, 1623

The eyes of all look to you,
   and you give them their food in due season.
You open your hand,
   satisfying the desire of every living thing.

PSALM 145:15–16

Giver of life and light, we acknowledge that apart from you we can do nothing.

28

"She would've been a good woman," said The Misfit, "if it had been somebody there to shoot her every minute of her life."

"A GOOD MAN IS HARD TO FIND" BY
FLANNERY O'CONNOR, 1955

For the time has come for judgment to begin with the household of God; if it begins with us, what will be the end for those who do not obey the gospel of God? And
"If it is hard for the righteous to be saved,
what will become of the ungodly and the sinners?"
Therefore, let those suffering in accordance with God's will entrust themselves to a faithful Creator, while continuing to do good.

1 PETER 4:17-19

O God, you know us inside and out. Help us to do the right thing, not just when the spotlight is on us, but in those quiet moments when only you and we know what we have done.

29

It was the last time she'd see the river from that window. The last time of anything has the poignancy of death itself. This that I see now, she thought, to see no more this way. Oh, the last time how clearly you see everything; as though a magnifying light had been turned on it. And you grieve because you hadn't held it tighter when you had it every day.

A TREE GROWS IN BROOKLYN BY BETTY SMITH, 1943

Yet you do not even know what tomorrow will bring. What is your life? For you are a mist that appears for a little while and then vanishes.

JAMES 4:14

Lord, in this fragile life, give me attentiveness to each day and gratitude for the gifts that surround me.

30

Nobody is incapable of doing a foolish thing. Nobody is incapable of doing a wrong thing.

AN IDEAL HUSBAND BY OSCAR WILDE, 1895

All have sinned and fall short of the glory of God; they are now justified by his grace as a gift, through the redemption that is in Christ Jesus.

ROMANS 3:23–24

Holy God, pick us up when we fall, forgive us our failures, and help us know that we are wrapped in the grace of your acceptance.

31

I understood that God does not wish men to live apart, and therefore he does not reveal to them what each one needs for himself; but he wishes them to live united, and therefore reveals to each of them what is necessary for all.

"WHAT MEN LIVE BY" BY LEO TOLSTOY, 1885

And let us consider how to provoke one another to love and good deeds, not neglecting to meet together, as is the habit of some, but encouraging one another, and all the more as you see the Day approaching.

HEBREWS 10:24-25

Our Father, help us not to isolate ourselves, but instead to find joy, strength, challenge, and help in community with others.

32

—‡——✳——‡—

Whatever life you lead you must put your soul in it—to make any sort of success in it, and from the moment you do that it ceases to be romance, I assure you: it becomes grim reality! And you can't always please yourself; you must sometimes please other people. That, I admit, you're very ready to do; but there's another thing that's still more important—you must often displease others. You must always be ready for that—you must never shrink from it. . . . You think we can escape disagreeable duties by taking romantic views—that's your great illusion, my dear. But we can't. You must be prepared on many occasions in life to please no one at all—not even yourself.

THE PORTRAIT OF A LADY BY HENRY JAMES, 1881

So let us not grow weary in doing what is right, for we will reap at harvest time, if we do not give up.

GALATIANS 6:9

Lord of all, give us the courage to tell the truth, even when it hurts us, and to seek out pathways of bold love and integrity.

One morning, as she was standing upright in the pool, splashing water between her shoulder-blades with a big sponge, something flashed through her mind that made her draw herself up and stand still until the water had quite dried upon her flushed skin. The stream and the broken pottery: what was any art but an effort to make a sheath, a mould in which to imprison for a moment the shining, elusive element which is life itself,—life hurrying past us and running away, too strong to stop, too sweet to lose?

THE SONG OF THE LARK BY WILLA CATHER, 1915

O LORD, what are human beings that you regard them,
    or mortals that you think of them?
They are like a breath;
    their days are like a passing shadow.

PSALM 144:3–4

Gracious God, thank you that you have given us the gifts of creation as well. We praise you and we bless you forever.

34

Say you are in the country; in some high land of lakes. Take almost any path you please, and ten to one it carries you down in a dale, and leaves you there by a pool in the stream. There is magic in it. Let the most absent-minded of men be plunged in his deepest reveries—stand that man on his legs, set his feet a-going, and he will infallibly lead you to water, if water there be in all that region. . . . Yes, as everyone knows, meditation and water are wedded forever.

MOBY-DICK BY HERMAN MELVILLE, 1851

In the beginning when God created the heavens and the earth, the earth was a formless void and darkness covered the face of the deep, while a wind from God swept over the face of the waters.

GENESIS 1:1–2

God of Mystery, make us attentive to your presence hovering over the world.

35

Conventionality is not morality. Self-righteousness is not religion. To attack the first is not to assail the last. To pluck the mask from the face of the Pharisee, is not to lift an impious hand to the Crown of Thorns. . . . Appearance should not be mistaken for truth; narrow human doctrines, that only tend to elate and magnify a few, should not be substituted for the world-redeeming creed of Christ.

FROM THE PREFACE TO *JANE EYRE* BY
CHARLOTTE BRONTË, 1847

And as Jesus sat at dinner in the house, many tax collectors and sinners came and were sitting with him and his disciples. When the Pharisees saw this, they said to his disciples, "Why does your teacher eat with tax collectors and sinners?" But when he heard this, he said, "Those who are well have no need of a physician, but those who are sick. Go and learn what this means, 'I desire mercy, not sacrifice.' For I have come to call not the righteous but sinners."

MATTHEW 9:10-13

Lord Christ, guard us from religion that elevates us above other people, and may your followers be marked by your humility, love, and service.

36

He smiled understandingly—much more than under-standingly. It was one of those rare smiles with a quality of eternal reassurance in it, that you may come across four or five times in life. It faced—or seemed to face—the whole eternal world for an instant, and then concentrated on you with an irresistible prejudice in your favor. It understood you just as far as you wanted to be understood, believed in you as you would like to believe in yourself, and assured you that it had precisely the impression of you that, at your best, you hoped to convey.

THE GREAT GATSBY BY F. SCOTT FITZGERALD, 1925

As he was setting out on a journey, a man ran up and knelt before him, and asked him, "Good Teacher, what must I do to inherit eternal life?" Jesus said to him, "Why do you call me good? No one is good but God alone. You know the commandments: 'You shall not murder; You shall not commit adultery; You shall not steal; You shall not bear false witness; You shall not defraud; Honor your father and mother.'" He said to him, "Teacher, I have kept all these since my youth." Jesus, looking at him, loved him and said, "You lack one thing; go, sell what you own, and give the money to the poor, and you will have treasure in heaven; then come, follow me."

MARK 10:17–21

Lord Jesus, you look at us, you see us, and you know us. Help us to live into the life you would have us live. Help us to follow you.

37

The benediction I would choose would be the one invoking *all* the names of God, Who by all accounts I'm buying spans the gamut.

FROM "ADVENTURES IN NEW TESTAMENT GREEK: *HAIRESIS*" BY SCOTT CAIRNS, 2002

I am the Alpha and the Omega, the first and the last, the beginning and the end.

REVELATION 22:13

Holy One, no name is sufficient to declare your glory and sound our praise. But accept our offering of thanks, our profession of love, and draw us ever closer to you, we pray.

38

Right is right, and wrong is wrong, and a body ain't got no business doing wrong when he ain't ignorant and knows better.

THE ADVENTURES OF HUCKLEBERRY FINN BY MARK TWAIN, 1884

This is the message we have heard from him and proclaim to you, that God is light and in him there is no darkness at all. If we say that we have fellowship with him while we are walking in darkness, we lie and do not do what is true; but if we walk in the light as he himself is in the light, we have fellowship with one another, and the blood of Jesus his Son cleanses us from all sin. If we say that we have no sin, we deceive ourselves, and the truth is not in us. If we confess our sins, he who is faithful and just will forgive us our sins and cleanse us from all unrighteousness. If we say that we have not sinned, we make him a liar, and his word is not in us.

1 JOHN 1:5-10

Give us, O God, the wisdom to know right from wrong, and the courage to do what is right, even when what is wrong is easier.

39

If all men abandon you and even drive you away by force, then when you are left alone, fall on the earth and kiss it; water it with your tears, and it will bring forth fruit even though no one has seen or heard you in your solitude. Believe to the end, even if all men went astray and you were left the only one faithful; bring your offering even then and praise God in your loneliness. And if two of you are gathered together—then there is a whole world, a world of living love.

THE BROTHERS KARAMAZOV BY FYODOR DOSTOEVSKY, 1880

For he delivers the needy when they call,
    the poor and those who have no helper.
He has pity on the weak and the needy,
    and saves the lives of the needy.

PSALM 72:12–13

God of Love, comfort us when we have been wronged. It is difficult not to spend hours thinking of how we might make the situation different, but we ask that you help us to leave solutions and restoration in your hands of justice and kindness.

40

Certain it is that whosoever hath his mind fraught with many thoughts, his wits and understanding do clarify and break up, in the communication and discoursing with another; he tosseth his thoughts more easily; he marshalleth them more orderly; he seeth how they look when they are turned into words.

"OF FRIENDSHIP" BY FRANCIS BACON, 1612

Anxiety weighs down the human heart,
  but a good word cheers it up.
The righteous gives good advice to friends.

PROVERBS 12:25–26A

Lord of Love, we thank you that you have given us friends to accompany us through difficulties, to comfort us in sorrow, and to impart wisdom in the midst of our unknowing.

41

The past remains hidden in clouds of memory. Still it returned us to memories from a thousand years before. Such a moment is the reason for a pilgrimage: infirmities forgotten, the ancients remembered, joyous tears trembled in my eyes.

NARROW ROAD TO THE INTERIOR BY MATSUO BASHŌ, 1694

When the LORD restored the fortunes of Zion,
    we were like those who dream.
Then our mouth was filled with laughter,
    and our tongue with shouts of joy;
then it was said among the nations,
    "The LORD has done great things for them."

PSALM 126:1–2

Holy Father, may our memories of your hand of love, guidance, and provision in our lives fill us each day with gratitude.

42

The fruitfulness of our little life, once we recognize it and live it as the life of the Beloved, is beyond anything we ourselves can imagine. One of the greatest acts of faith is to believe that the few years we live on this earth are like a little seed planted in a very rich soil. For this seed to bear fruit, it must die.

LIFE OF THE BELOVED BY HENRI NOUWEN, 1992

Very truly, I tell you, unless a grain of wheat falls into the earth and dies, it remains just a single grain; but if it dies, it bears much fruit.

JOHN 12:24

God who holds the power over life and death, give us faith to believe that you are able to bring fruitfulness from the places in our lives that seem dead and dormant.

43

"Where there is great love there are always miracles," he said at length. "One might say that an apparition is human vision corrected by divine love. I do not see you as you really are, Joseph; I see you through my affection for you. The Miracles of the Church seem to me to rest not so much upon faces or voices or healing power coming suddenly near to us from afar off, but upon our perceptions being made finer, so that for a moment our eyes can see and our ears can hear what is there about us always."

DEATH COMES FOR THE ARCHBISHOP BY WILLA CATHER, 1927

Seek the LORD and his strength;
    seek his presence continually.
Remember the wonderful works he has done,
    his miracles, and the judgments he has uttered.

PSALM 105:4–5

Holy One of Miracles, help us to see and know the wonders with which you surround us every day.

44

It may be misery not to sing at all,
  And to go silent through the brimming day;
It may be misery never to be loved,
But deeper griefs than these beset the way.

To sing the perfect song,
And by a half-tone lost the key,
There the potent sorrow, there the grief,
The pale, sad staring of Life's Tragedy.

FROM "LIFE'S TRAGEDY"
BY PAUL LAURENCE DUNBAR, 1903

For in much wisdom is much vexation,
and those who increase knowledge increase sorrow.

ECCLESIASTES 1:18

O Lord, meet us in our tender places of disappointment, loss, and grief.

45

Our joys were dearer because we saw their end; they were keener because we felt, to its fullest extent, their value; they were purer because their essence was sympathy—as a meteor is brighter than a star, did the felicity of this winter contain in itself the extracted delights of a long, long life.

THE LAST MAN BY MARY SHELLEY, 1826

Lord, let me know my end,
    and what is the measure of my days;
    let me know how fleeting my life is.

PSALM 39:4

Our Father, let us recognize the numerous gifts that we have been given, and fill our days with gratitude.

46

Death may beget life, but oppression can beget nothing other than itself.

A TALE OF TWO CITIES BY CHARLES DICKENS, 1859

Again I saw all the oppressions that are practiced under the sun. Look, the tears of the oppressed—with no one to comfort them! On the side of their oppressors there was power—with no one to comfort them.

ECCLESIASTES 4:1

God of Comfort, see the tears of the oppressed, and be their Redeemer. Humble those who misuse and abuse their power, and lift up the lowly.

47

It's a good place to live; there's a lot to think about. The creeks—Tinker and Carvin's—are an active mystery, fresh every minute. Theirs is the mystery of the continuous creation and all that providence implies: the uncertainty of vision, the horror of the fixed, the dissolution of the present, the intricacy of beauty, the pressure of fecundity, the elusiveness of the free, and the flawed nature of perfection.

PILGRIM AT TINKER CREEK BY ANNIE DILLARD, 1974

For I will pour water on the thirsty land,
   and streams on the dry ground;
I will pour my spirit upon your descendants,
   and my blessing on your offspring.

ISAIAH 44:3

Lord Christ, may your living water revive, sustain, and renew us as we walk through this fragile life.

48

So I am content to tell my simple story, without trying to make things seem better than they were; dreading nothing, indeed, but falsity, which, in spite of one's best efforts, there is reason to dread. Falsehood is so easy, truth so difficult.

ADAM BEDE BY GEORGE ELIOT, 1859

Never be rash with your mouth, nor let your heart be quick to utter a word before God, for God is in heaven, and you upon earth; therefore let your words be few.

ECCLESIASTES 5:2

Our Lord, may our words be true, thoughtful, kind, and filled with humble love.

49

"Don't you know who is the King of Beasts? Aslan is a lion—*the* Lion, the great Lion."

"Ooh!" said Susan, "I'd thought he was a man. Is he—quite safe? I shall feel rather nervous about meeting a lion."

"That you will, dearie, and no mistake," said Mrs. Beaver, "if there's anyone who can appear before Aslan without their knees knocking, they're either braver than most or else just silly."

"Then he isn't safe?" said Lucy.

"Safe?" said Mr. Beaver. "Don't you hear what Mrs. Beaver tells you? Who said anything about safe? 'Course he isn't safe. But he's good."

THE LION, THE WITCH, AND THE WARDROBE BY C. S. LEWIS, 1950

For thus says the high and lofty one
    who inhabits eternity, whose name is Holy:
I dwell in the high and holy place,
    and also with those who are contrite and humble in spirit,
to revive the spirit of the humble,
    and to revive the heart of the contrite.

ISAIAH 57:15

Mighty God, Lion of Judah, how could one so holy meet us in our lowliness? How can your power be so tender?

50

A mong other things, you'll find that you're not the first person who was ever confused and frightened and even sickened by human behavior. . . . Many, many men have been just as troubled morally and spiritually as you are right now. Happily, some of them kept records of their troubles. You'll learn from them—if you want to. Just as someday, if you have something to offer, someone will learn something from you. It's a beautiful reciprocal arrangement. And it isn't education. It's history. It's poetry.

THE CATCHER IN THE RYE BY J. D. SALINGER, 1951

Simon, Simon, listen! Satan has demanded to sift all of you like wheat, but I have prayed for you that your own faith may not fail; and you, when once you have turned back, strengthen your brothers.

LUKE 22:31–32

Lord God, we are weak and troubled. Meet us in our need, that we might meet those in need around us.

51

You, created only a little lower than
  The angels, have crouched too long in
The bruising darkness,
Have lain too long
Face down in ignorance.

FROM "ON THE PULSE OF MORNING"
BY MAYA ANGELOU, 1993

Justice, and only justice, you shall pursue, so that you may live and occupy the land that the LORD your God is giving you.

DEUTERONOMY 16:20

You have told us, O God, the good you would have us do. Forgive us when we shrink from doing it. Grant us courage to pursue justice, now and from now on.

52

To love another person is to see the face of God.

LES MISÉRABLES BY VICTOR HUGO, 1862

So God created humankind in his image,
    in the image of God he created them;
    male and female he created them.

GENESIS 1:27

*Lord our God, may we not forget that all of us, no matter
how different we are, bear your divine image and are precious
in your sight.*

53

The logic of worldly success rests on a fallacy: the strange error that our perfection depends on the thoughts and opinions and applause of other men! A weird life it is, indeed, to be living always in somebody else's imagination, as if that were the only place in which one could at last become real!

THE SEVEN STOREY MOUNTAIN BY THOMAS MERTON, 1948

The thief comes only to steal and kill and destroy. I came that they may have life, and have it abundantly.

JOHN 10:10

Holy Father, may we not be robbed of our joy by thinking always of how others perceive us, and may we find our realness in being your children.

54

But oh! for the woods, the flowers
 Of natural, sweet perfume,
The heartening, summer showers
And the smiling shrubs in bloom,
Dust-free, dew-tinted at morn,
The fresh and life-giving air,
The billowing waves of corn
And the birds' notes rich and clear:—
For a man-machine toil-tired
May crave beauty too—though he's hired.

FROM "JOY IN THE WOODS"
BY CLAUDE MCKAY, 1920

Those who oppress the poor insult their Maker,
 but those who are kind to the needy honor him.

PROVERBS 14:31

Holy Lord, we sorrow for human beings who are oppressed and enslaved by other human beings. May we honor rather than insult you through our actions of justice and love.

55

I wanted you to see what real courage is, instead of getting the idea that courage is a man with a gun in his hand. It's knowing you're licked before you begin but you begin anyway and you see it through no matter what. You rarely win, but sometimes you do.

TO KILL A MOCKINGBIRD BY HARPER LEE, 1960

David said further to his son Solomon, "Be strong and of good courage, and act. Do not be afraid or dismayed; for the LORD God, my God, is with you."

1 CHRONICLES 28:20

Holy Father, fill our hearts with courage, even when the forces against us seem too strong or complex to contend with.

For being a foreigner, Ashima is beginning to realize, is a sort of lifelong pregnancy—a perpetual wait, a constant burden, a continuous feeling out of sorts. It is an ongoing responsibility, a parenthesis in what had once been an ordinary life, only to discover that previous life has vanished, replaced by something more complicated and demanding. Like pregnancy, being a foreigner, Ashima believes, is something that elicits the same curiosity from strangers, the same combination of pity and respect.

THE NAMESAKE BY JHUMPA LAHIRI, 2003

Hear my prayer, O LORD,
    and give ear to my cry;
    do not hold your peace at my tears.
For I am your passing guest,
    an alien, like all my forebears.

PSALM 39:12

God of all, help us to understand that we have all been strangers in a strange land and to love and serve each other without reserve.

57

Christianity is always out of fashion because it is always sane; and all fashions are mild insanities. When Italy is mad on art the Church seems too Puritanical; when England is mad on Puritanism the Church seems too artistic. . . . The Church always seems to be behind the times, when it is really beyond the times; it is waiting till the last fad shall have seen its last summer. It keeps the key of a permanent virtue.

THE BALL AND THE CROSS BY G. K. CHESTERTON, 1909

Although I am the very least of all the saints, this grace was given to me to bring to the Gentiles the news of the boundless riches of Christ, and to make everyone see what is the plan of the mystery hidden for ages in God who created all things; so that through the church the wisdom of God in its rich variety might now be made known to the rulers and authorities in the heavenly places.

EPHESIANS 3:8–10

Lord Christ, may we elevate you alone, even as trends and language and ideas change and shift. We confess your holy life and redemption as the mystery hidden for ages in God.

58

The silence of the Plains, this great unpeopled landscape of earth and sky, is much like the silence one finds in a monastery, an unfathomable silence that has the power to re-form you.

DAKOTA: A SPIRITUAL GEOGRAPHY
BY KATHLEEN NORRIS, 1993

Be still, and know that I am God!
   I am exalted among the nations,
   I am exalted in the earth.

PSALM 46:10

Holy God, help us to be silent and to know your presence, and may that knowledge shape and reshape us into the people you would have us be.

59

I see the wrong that round me lies,
  I feel the guilt within;
I hear, with groan and travail-cries,
The world confess its sin.
Yet, in the maddening maze of things,
And tossed by storm and flood,
To one fixed trust my spirit clings;
I know that God is good!

FROM "THE ETERNAL GOODNESS" BY
JOHN GREENLEAF WHITTIER, 1865

Once God has spoken;
    twice have I heard this:
that power belongs to God,
    and steadfast love belongs to you, O Lord.
For you repay to all
    according to their work.

PSALM 62:11–12

*God who does not change, we look to you to be our steadiness,
our true anchor, our hope.*

60

The Christian needs another Christian who speaks God's Word to him. He needs him again and again when he becomes uncertain and discouraged, for by himself he cannot help himself without belying the truth. He needs his brother man as a bearer and proclaimer of the divine word of salvation.

LIFE TOGETHER BY DIETRICH BONHOEFFER, 1939

Let the word of Christ dwell in you richly; teach and admonish one another in all wisdom; and with gratitude in your hearts sing psalms, hymns, and spiritual songs to God.

COLOSSIANS 3:16

Triune God, may we embrace our need for relationships, for support, and for the belief of others. We are made in your image, our God of relationality and love.

61

It contributes greatly towards a man's moral and intellectual health, to be brought into habits of companionship with individuals unlike himself, who care little for his pursuits, and whose sphere and abilities he must go out of himself to appreciate.

INTRODUCTION TO *THE SCARLET LETTER*
BY NATHANIEL HAWTHORNE, 1850

For just as the body is one and has many members, and all the members of the body, though many, are one body, so it is with Christ. For in the one Spirit we were all baptized into one body—Jews or Greeks, slaves or free—and we are all made to drink of one Spirit.

1 CORINTHIANS 12:12-13

Lord Christ, teach us to honor and value others for their differences. May we be ready to learn from those who are not like us.

62

"Is that all you have to say?" asked Mr. Brand.

"Yes, it's all—but it will bear a good deal of thinking of."

Felix went with him to the garden-gate, and watched him slowly walk away into the thickening twilight with a relaxed rigidity that tried to rectify itself. "He is offended, excited, bewildered, perplexed—and enchanted!" Felix said to himself, "That's a capital mixture."

THE EUROPEANS BY HENRY JAMES, 1878

The mind of the righteous ponders how to answer,
    but the mouth of the wicked pours out evil.

PROVERBS 15:28

Holy Father, let our words be thoughtful, our responses wise, our actions fitting.

63

L ove ain't somethin' lak uh grindstone dat's de same thing everywhere and do de same thing tuh everything it touch. Love is lak de sea. It's uh movin' thing, but still and all, it takes its shape from de shore it meets, and it's different with every shore.

THEIR EYES WERE WATCHING GOD BY
ZORA NEALE HURSTON, 1937

[Love] bears all things, believes all things, hopes all things, endures all things.
Love never ends.

1 CORINTHIANS 13:7–8A

Holy God, impress upon us the wideness, the depth, and the mystery of your great love.

64

Holiness has most often been revealed to me in the exquisite pun of the first syllable, in holes— in not enough help, in brokenness, mess. High holy places, with ethereal sounds and stained glass, can massage my illusion of holiness, but in holes and lostness I can pick up the light of small ordinary progress, newly made moments flecked like pepper into the slog and the disruptions.

PLAN B: FURTHER THOUGHTS ON FAITH BY ANNE LAMOTT, 2005

When you search for me, you will find me; if you seek me with all your heart.

JEREMIAH 29:13

Holy One, help us to see the holiness in the brokenness, the holiness in the ordinary, and to give thanks for your presence in all places and times.

65

Sunshine let it be or frost,
  Storm or calm, as Thou shalt choose;
Though Thine every gift were lost,
Thee Thyself we could not lose.

"AFTER ST. AUGUSTINE" BY
MARY ELIZABETH COLERIDGE, 1908

I, I am he who comforts you;
  why then are you afraid of a mere mortal who must die,
  a human being who fades like grass?

ISAIAH 51:12

Lord, we thank you for your nearness to us, and that whether or not we feel that nearness, still your presence abides with us.

66

As to the sentence of the judge, I'm not one to know. . . . If I, Finn, was judge I'd know well enough though. I'd sentence him to have mercy on himself. I'd sentence him less to strive for the glory of God than just to let it swell his sails if it can.

BRENDAN BY FREDERICK BUECHNER, 1987

I lie down and sleep;
    I wake again, for the LORD sustains me.

PSALM 3:5

Holy Father, may we depend on you to sustain us through the joys and sorrows of our lives, and to carry us through all things with your mercy.

Suffering has been stronger than all other teaching, and has taught me to understand what your heart used to be. I have been bent and broken, but—I hope—into a better shape.

GREAT EXPECTATIONS BY CHARLES DICKENS, 1860–61

And after you have suffered for a little while, the God of all grace, who has called you to his eternal glory in Christ, will himself restore, support, strengthen, and establish you.

1 PETER 5:10

Christ our Suffering Servant, we thank you that you know us intimately in the midst of our suffering, and that you do not abandon us in the face of adversity.

68

Under his pillow lay the Gospels. He took the book out mechanically. It belonged to her, it was the same one from which she had read to him about the raising of Lazarus. At the beginning of his hard labor he had thought she would hound him with religion, would be forever talking about the Gospels and forcing books on him. But to his greatest amazement, she never once spoke of it, never once even offered him the Gospels. . . . But here begins a new account, the account of a man's gradual renewal, the account of his gradual regeneration, his gradual transition from one world to another, his acquaintance with a new, hitherto completely unknown reality.

CRIME AND PUNISHMENT BY FYODOR DOSTOEVSKY, 1866

But in your hearts sanctify Christ as Lord. Always be ready to make your defense to anyone who demands from you an accounting for the hope that is in you; yet do it with gentleness and reverence.

1 PETER 3:15–16A

Christ our Lord, give us the wisdom to discern the needs of those around us, to be attentive to the hungers of their hearts so our words, actions, and even our silences may greet them with your love.

My life is like a faded leaf,
My harvest dwindled to a husk:
Truly my life is void and brief
And tedious in the barren dusk;
My life is like a frozen thing,
No bud nor greenness can I see:
Yet rise it shall—the sap of Spring;
O Jesus, rise in me.

FROM "A BETTER RESURRECTION"
BY CHRISTINA ROSSETTI, 1862

As a father has compassion for his children,
    so the LORD has compassion for those who fear him.
For he knows how we were made;
    he remembers that we are dust.

PSALM 103:13–14

Our Lord Christ, we praise you for your compassion on our human frailty, and for your miraculous promise to bring new life into the midst of our weakness.

70

Childhood has no forebodings; but then, it is soothed by no memories of outlived sorrow.

THE MILL ON THE FLOSS BY GEORGE ELIOT, 1860

I cry aloud to God,
  aloud to God, that he may hear me.
. . . .
I will call to mind the deeds of the LORD;
  I will remember your wonders of old.

PSALM 77:1, 11

Father, we remember the ways you have brought us through hardships, heartache, pain, and loss. We thank you for never leaving us nor forsaking us.

71

It is not allowable to love the Creation according to the purposes one has for it, any more than it is allowable to love one's neighbor in order to borrow his tools. . . . The Creator's love for the Creation is mysterious precisely because it does not conform to human purposes. The wild ass and the wild lilies are loved by God for their own sake and yet they are part of a pattern that we must love because it includes us. This is a pattern that humans can understand well enough to respect and preserve, though they cannot "control" it or hope to understand it completely.

"THE GIFT OF GOOD LAND" BY WENDELL BERRY, 1981

> For the LORD your God is bringing you into a good land, a land with flowing streams, with springs and underground waters welling up in valleys and hills, a land of wheat and barley, of vines and fig trees and pomegranates, a land of olive trees and honey, a land where you may eat bread without scarcity, where you will lack nothing.

DEUTERONOMY 8:7–9A

Lord of all, you have given us abundant gifts on this earth. Forgive us for treating them lightly, and teach us to live with reverence and care for all you have made.

72

Elinor had not needed . . . to be assured of the injustice to which her sister was often led in her opinion of others, by the irritable refinement of her own mind, and the too great importance placed by her on the delicacies of a strong sensibility and the graces of a polished manner. Like half the rest of the world, if more than half there be that are clever and good, Marianne, with excellent abilities and an excellent disposition, was neither reasonable nor candid. She expected from other people the same opinions and feelings as her own, and she judged of their motives by the immediate effect of their actions on herself.

SENSE AND SENSIBILITY BY JANE AUSTEN, 1811

I am sending you out like sheep into the midst of wolves; so be wise as serpents and innocent as doves.

MATTHEW 10:16

Lord, grant me discernment and understanding, caution and gentility, and the wisdom to use them in ways that honor you.

73

After all, people may really have in them some vocation which is not quite plain to themselves, may they not? They may seem idle and weak because they are growing. We should be very patient with each other, I think.

MIDDLEMARCH BY GEORGE ELIOT, 1871–72

I therefore, the prisoner in the Lord, beg you to lead a life worthy of the calling to which you have been called, with all humility and gentleness, with patience, bearing with one another in love, making every effort to maintain the unity of the Spirit in the bond of peace.

EPHESIANS 4:1–3

Our God, every day you are long-suffering with us, patient in our weakness and sin. May we extend to others the generosity we continually receive.

74

I t is unearned love—the love that goes before, that greets us on the way. It's the help you receive when you have no bright ideas left, when you are empty and desperate and have discovered that your best thinking and most charming charm have failed you. Grace is the light or electricity or juice or breeze that takes you from that isolated place and puts you with others who are as startled and embarrassed and eventually grateful as you are to be there.

TRAVELING MERCIES: SOME THOUGHTS ON FAITH BY ANNE LAMOTT, 1999

To those who have received a faith as precious as ours through the righteousness of our God and Savior Jesus Christ:
May grace and peace be yours in abundance in the knowledge of God and of Jesus our Lord.

2 PETER 1:1B–2

God of Grace, take us from our place of isolation and shame and bring us to the place of righteousness, abundance, and gratitude.

75

The birth of my own babies . . . shows me that the power which staggers with its splendor is a power of love, particular love. . . . We are surely one of his failures. He loved us enough to come to us, and we didn't want him, and this incredible visit ended in total failure, and this failure gives me cause to question all failure, and all success. And even after failure he continues to be concerned for us. We can, if we will, recognize him as he is manifested in love, total, giving love. And I believe that in one way or another we are all meant to receive him as Mary did.

THE IRRATIONAL SEASON BY MADELEINE L'ENGLE, 1977

The angel said to her, "Do not be afraid, Mary, for you have found favor with God. And now, you will conceive in your womb and bear a son, and you will name him Jesus. He will be great, and will be called the Son of the Most High, and the Lord God will give to him the throne of his ancestor David. He will reign over the house of Jacob forever, and of his kingdom there will be no end."

LUKE 1:30–33

Holy Father, may our hearts mirror Mary's, with a willingness to believe in the impossible and world-shifting realities of a world inhabited by God.

76

Each one of us here today will at one time in our lives look upon a loved one who is in need and ask the same question: We are willing to help, Lord, but what, if anything, is needed? For it is true we can seldom help those closest to us. Either we don't know what part of ourselves to give or, more often than not, the part we have to give is not wanted. And so it is those we live with and should know who elude us. But we can still love them—we can love completely without complete understanding.

A RIVER RUNS THROUGH IT AND OTHER STORIES BY NORMAN MACLEAN, 1976

If I speak in the tongues of mortals and of angels, but do not have love, I am a noisy gong or a clanging cymbal. And if I have prophetic powers, and understand all mysteries and all knowledge, and if I have all faith, so as to remove mountains, but do not have love, I am nothing. If I give away all my possessions, and if I hand over my body so that I may boast, but do not have love, I gain nothing.

Love is patient; love is kind; love is not envious or boastful or arrogant or rude. It does not insist on its own way; it is not irritable or resentful; it does not rejoice in wrongdoing, but rejoices in the truth.

1 CORINTHIANS 13:1-6

We are willing to help, Lord; show us what is needed, and give us the strength to love with all our hearts.

77

There is no one to tell us what might have been. We weep over the might have been, but there is no might have been. There never was. It is supposed to be true that those who do not know history are condemned to repeat it. I don't believe knowing can save us. What is constant in history is greed and foolishness and a love of blood and this is a thing that even God—who knows all that can be known—seems powerless to change.

ALL THE PRETTY HORSES BY CORMAC MCCARTHY, 1992

Daniel said:
"Blessed be the name of God from age to age,
    for wisdom and power are his.
He changes times and seasons,
    deposes kings and sets up kings;
he gives wisdom to the wise
    and knowledge to those who have understanding."

DANIEL 2:20–21

All-Knowing God of past and future, help us live into the present, secure that what you have designed for us is the reality we may live into and embrace.

78

Most of us creatures of flesh and blood know what that terrible feeling of suspense, of dread, with which we approach a crisis in our fate. It is indefinable, but comes alike strong and weak, bold and timid. Such a crisis Maxwell felt was approaching in the fate of Winona and himself. Therein we recognize the mesmeric force which holds mankind in an eternal brotherhood.

WINONA: A TALE OF NEGRO LIFE IN THE SOUTH
AND SOUTHWEST BY PAULINE HOPKINS, 1902

> In God, whose word I praise,
>   in God I trust; I am not afraid;
>   what can flesh do to me?
> . . . .
> You have kept count of my tossings;
>   put my tears in your bottle.
>   Are they not in your record?

PSALM 56:4, 8

Holy God, in the face of situations that make us fearful and overwhelmed, we ask that you would be near to us and give us the strength we need to stand up under hardship.

79

Nothing can be sadder or more profound than to see a thousand things for the first and last time. To journey is to be born and die each minute. . . . All the elements of life are in constant flight from us, with darkness and clarity intermingled, the vision and the eclipse; we look and hasten, reaching out our hands to clutch; every happening is a bend in the road . . . and suddenly we have grown old.

LES MISÉRABLES BY VICTOR HUGO, 1862

He has made everything suitable for its time; moreover he has put a sense of past and future into their minds, yet they cannot find out what God has done from the beginning to the end.

ECCLESIASTES 3:11

Author of Life, we confess the mystery that our lives are fragile and fleeting, while also filled with profound meaning and depth of love.

80

I put the chocolate in my mouth, letting it soften until the last possible moment, and then as I chewed it slowly, I prayed that Mr. Pirzada's family was safe and sound. I had never prayed for anything before, had never been taught or told to, but I decided, given the circumstances, that it was something I should do. That night when I went to the bathroom I only pretended to brush my teeth, for I feared that I would somehow rinse the prayer out as well. I wet the brush and rearranged the tube of paste to prevent my parents from asking any questions, and fell asleep with sugar on my tongue.

"WHEN MR. PIRZADA CAME TO DINE" BY JHUMPA LAHIRI, 1999

Hear my prayer, O God;
   give ear to the words of my mouth.

PSALM 54:2

Teach us to pray, O Lord, so that the words of our mouths and the meditation of our hearts may be satisfying to you.

81

Various are the roads of man. He who follows and compares them will see strange figures emerge, figures which seem to belong to that great cipher which we discern written everywhere, in wings, eggshells, clouds and snow, in crystals and in stone formations, on ice-covered waters, on the inside and outside of mountains, of plants, beasts and men, in the lights of heaven, on scored disks of pitch or glass or in iron filings round a magnet, and in strange conjunctures of chance.

THE NOVICES OF SAIS BY NOVALIS, 1802

For as the rain and the snow come down from heaven,
    and do not return there until they have watered the earth,
making it bring forth and sprout,
    giving seed to the sower and bread to the eater,
so shall my word be that goes out from my mouth;
    it shall not return to me empty,
but it shall accomplish that which I purpose,
    and succeed in the thing for which I sent it.

ISAIAH 55:10–11

O Lord, we see your hand on the patterns and beauties and mysteries around us, and we thank you for the mark of holiness on the world.

82

After that hard winter, one could not get enough of the nimble air. Every morning I wakened with a fresh consciousness that winter was over. There were none of the signs of spring for which I used to watch in Virginia, no budding woods or blooming gardens. There was only—spring itself; the throb of it, the light restlessness, the vital essence of it everywhere: in the sky, in the swift clouds, in the pale sunshine, and in the warm, high wind—rising suddenly, sinking suddenly, impulsive and playful.

MY ÁNTONIA BY WILLA CATHER, 1918

My beloved speaks and says to me:
"Arise, my love, my fair one,
    and come away;
for now the winter is past,
    the rain is over and gone."

SONG OF SOLOMON 2:10–11

Our Lord, after times of dormancy and brittleness, we hope for new life, for the return of delight, abundance, and expectation.

83

Before I can live with other folks I've got to live with myself. The one thing that doesn't abide by majority rule is a person's conscience.

TO KILL A MOCKINGBIRD BY HARPER LEE, 1960

Keep your heart with all vigilance,
    for from it flow the springs of life.
. . . .
Let your eyes look directly forward,
    and your gaze be straight before you.
Keep straight the path of your feet,
    and all your ways will be sure.

PROVERBS 4:23, 25–26

God of Truth, give me boldness to stand for the cause of justice and courage to act with integrity despite the cost.

84

There is a loneliness that can be rocked. Arms crossed, knees drawn up, holding, holding on, this motion, unlike a ship's, smooths and contains the rocker. It's an inside kind—wrapped tight like skin. Then there is the loneliness that roams. No rocking can hold it down. It is alive. On its own. A dry and spreading thing that makes the sound of one's own feet going seem to come from a far-off place.

BELOVED BY TONI MORRISON, 1987

When you pass through the waters, I will be with you;
    and through the rivers, they shall not overwhelm you;
when you walk through fire you shall not be burned,
    and the flame shall not consume you.
For I am the LORD your God,
    the Holy One of Israel, your Savior.

ISAIAH 43:2–3A

Holy Lord, in our loneliness, in our fear, in the places where we feel we may not be able to persevere, meet us, and visit us with your salvation.

85

We cannot arrive at the perfect possession of God in this life, and that is why we are travelling and in darkness. But we already possess Him by grace, and therefore in that sense we have arrived and are dwelling in light. But oh! How far have I to go to find You in Whom I have already arrived!

THE SEVEN STOREY MOUNTAIN BY THOMAS MERTON, 1948

For all things are yours, whether Paul or Apollos or Cephas or the world or life or death or the present or the future—all belong to you, and you belong to Christ, and Christ belongs to God.

1 CORINTHIANS 3:21B-23

Holy God, give me perseverance in faith, patience in hope, and trust in your promise.

86

I am saying that a journey is called that because you cannot know what you will discover on the journey, what you will do with what you find, or what you find will do to you.

I AM NOT YOUR NEGRO BY JAMES BALDWIN, 2017

Now the LORD said to Abram, "Go from your country and your kindred and your father's house to the land that I will show you. I will make of you a great nation, and I will bless you, and make your name great, so that you will be a blessing. I will bless those who bless you, and the one who curses you I will curse; and in you all the families of the earth shall be blessed."

GENESIS 12:1-3

Holy One, walk with us on the journey you have planned for us, bless us, and strengthen us so that we may arrive at the end of that journey transformed.

87

G od is of a kind to love the world extravagantly, wondrously, and the world is of a kind to be worth, which is not to say worthy of, this pained and rapturous love. This is the essence of the story that forever eludes telling. It lives in the world not as myth or history but as a saturating light, a light so brilliant that it hides its source, to borrow an image from another good old hymn.

"WONDROUS LOVE" BY MARILYNNE ROBINSON, 2012

For I am convinced that neither death, nor life, nor angels, nor rulers, nor things present, nor things to come, nor powers, nor height, nor depth, nor anything else in all creation, will be able to separate us from the love of God in Christ Jesus our Lord.

ROMANS 8:38–39

Christ our Lord, we praise you for your great love, beyond all we can conceive, deeper than all we imagine!

88

"People have forgotten this truth," the fox said. "But you mustn't forget it. You become responsible forever for what you've tamed. You're responsible for your rose."

THE LITTLE PRINCE BY ANTOINE DE SAINT-EXUPÉRY, 1943

The righteous know the needs of their animals,
    but the mercy of the wicked is cruel.

PROVERBS 12:10

Lord of all creation, give us humble care for your world, and may we live not with greed and entitlement but with attention and reverence.

89

If then my heart cannot endure the blaze
  Of beauties infinite that blind these eyes,
    Nor yet can bear to be from you divided,

What fate is mine? Who guides or guards my ways,
  Seeing my soul, so lost and ill-betided,
    Burns in your presence, in your absence dies?

FROM SONNET XXIX, "LOVE'S DILEMMA,"
BY MICHELANGELO BUONARROTI, 1623

You hem me in, behind and before,
  and lay your hand upon me.
Such knowledge is too wonderful for me;
  it is so high that I cannot attain it.

PSALM 139:5–6

Holy God, dwelling beyond us and intimately near to us,
we are humbled by your abundant presence.

90

S eldom, very seldom, does complete truth belong to any
human disclosure; seldom can it happen that something
is not a little disguised, or a little mistaken.

EMMA BY JANE AUSTEN, 1815

O God, you know my folly;
the wrongs I have done are not hidden from you.

PSALM 69:5

*Our Father, so often it can be hard to say what we really mean,
to hear what is really said. In our weakness, we give thanks that
you know each of us more fully than we know ourselves.*

91

I've known rivers:
    I've known rivers ancient as the world and older than the
    flow of human blood in human veins.
My soul has grown deep like the rivers.

"THE NEGRO SPEAKS OF RIVERS"
BY LANGSTON HUGHES, 1921

But there the Lord in majesty will be for us
    a place of broad rivers and streams,
where no galley with oars can go,
    nor stately ship can pass.
For the Lord is our judge, the Lord is our ruler,
    the Lord is our king; he will save us.

ISAIAH 33:21-22

Holy God, we remember with grief the horrors of slavery, past and present. Only you can heal our land.

92

You hammer against the walls of your house. You tap the walls lightly, everywhere. After giving many years' attention to these things, you know what to listen for. Some of the walls are bearing walls; they have to stay, or everything will fall down. Other walls can go with impunity; you can hear the difference. Unfortunately, it is often a bearing wall that has to go. It cannot be helped. There is only one solution, which appalls you, but there it is. Knock it out. Duck.

THE WRITING LIFE BY ANNIE DILLARD, 1989

God is our refuge and strength,
   a very present help in trouble.
Therefore we will not fear, though the earth should change,
   though the mountains shake in the heart of the sea.

PSALM 46:1–2

Unchanging God, so much around us does not hold steady, and that unsteadiness makes us afraid. Give us courage in the face of uncertainty and bold trust in your loving presence.

93

I have a lot of faith. But I am also afraid a lot, and have no real certainty about anything. I remembered something Father Tom had told me—that the opposite of faith is not doubt, but certainty. Certainty is missing the point entirely. Faith includes noticing the mess, the emptiness and discomfort, and letting it be there until some light returns.

PLAN B: FURTHER THOUGHTS ON FAITH BY ANNE LAMOTT, 2005

The Lord is my rock, my fortress, and my deliverer,
　　my God, my rock, in whom I take refuge,
my shield and the horn of my salvation,
　　my stronghold and my refuge,
　　my savior; you save me from violence.
I call upon the LORD, who is worthy to be praised,
　　and I am saved from my enemies.

2 SAMUEL 22:2–4

Grant us faith, Lord, real faith that sees the world as it is, but also sees the world as you would have it be.

94

They had to knock loudly before Silas heard them; but when he did come to the door he showed no impatience, as he would once have done, at a visit that had been unasked for and unexpected. Formerly, his heart had been as a locked casket with its treasure inside; but now the casket was empty, and the lock was broken. Left groping in the darkness, with his prop utterly gone, Silas had inevitably a sense, though a dull and half-despairing one, that if any help came to him it must come from without; and there was a slight stirring of expectation at the sight of his fellow-men, a faint consciousness of dependence on their goodwill.

SILAS MARNER BY GEORGE ELIOT, 1861

For I am longing to see you so that I may share with you some spiritual gift to strengthen you—or rather so that we may be mutually encouraged by each other's faith, both yours and mine.

ROMANS 1:11–12

O Lord, make our hearts open to receive the encouragement and love of others, especially when it feels like it would be safer to bear our burdens alone.

95

I sometimes think there's two sides to the commandment; and that we may say, "Let others do unto you, as you would do unto them," for pride often prevents our giving others a great deal of pleasure, in not letting them be kind, when their hearts are longing to help.

MARY BARTON BY ELIZABETH GASKELL, 1848

When pride comes, then comes disgrace;
  but wisdom is with the humble.

PROVERBS 11:2

Lord, destroy my pride that I may live only for you.

96

Life is easy to chronicle, but bewildering to practice.

A ROOM WITH A VIEW BY E. M. FORSTER, 1908

Even though I walk through the darkest valley,
    I fear no evil;
for you are with me;
    your rod and your staff—
    they comfort me.

PSALM 23:4

Lord Christ, our Good Shepherd, through all we face, days of confusion and distress, or joy and peace, we look to you to be our guide.

97

—⟡— ✳ —⟡—

Her stories give them something to talk about and to conjecture about, cut off as they are from the restless currents of the world. The many naked little sandbars which lie between Venice and the mainland, in the seemingly stagnant water of the lagoons, are made habitable and wholesome only because, every night, a foot and a half of tide creeps in from the sea and winds its fresh brine up through all that network of shining waterways. So, into all the little settlements of quiet people, tidings of what their boys and girls are doing in the world bring real refreshment; bring to the old, memories, and to the young, dreams.

THE SONG OF THE LARK BY WILLA CATHER, 1915

Let them thank the LORD for his steadfast love,
 for his wonderful works to humankind.
For he satisfies the thirsty,
 and the hungry he fills with good things.
. . . .
He turns a desert into pools of water,
 a parched land into springs of water.

PSALM 107:8-9, 35

We are grateful, O God, for the stories of your steadfast love, and for life.

98

Who would have thought my shrivel'd heart
    Could have recover'd greenness? It was gone
Quite under ground; as flowers depart
To see their mother-root, when they have blown;
Where they together
All the hard weather,
Dead to the world, keep house unknown.

These are thy wonders, Lord of power,
Killing and quickning, bringing down to hell
And up to heaven in an houre;
Making a chiming of a passing-bell.
We say amiss
This or that is:
Thy word is all, if we could spell.

FROM "THE FLOWER" BY GEORGE HERBERT, 1633

Do not forsake me, O LORD;
    O my God, do not be far from me.

PSALM 38:21

Our Father, when we have nothing left, we look to you.
Speak us into life.

The difference between treason and patriotism is only a matter of dates.

THE COUNT OF MONTE CRISTO BY ALEXANDRE DUMAS, 1844–45

Since, then, we have such a hope, we act with great boldness.

2 CORINTHIANS 3:12

Our Lord who is above the rulers and powers of this world, grant us wisdom, courage, and integrity to critique or to celebrate the systems around us when circumstances call for it. May we serve your kingdom.

100

One of the surprises of her unoccupied state was the discovery that time, when it is left to itself and no definite demands are made on it, cannot be trusted to move at any recognized pace. Usually it loiters; but just when one has come to count upon its slowness, it may suddenly break into a wild irrational gallop.

THE HOUSE OF MIRTH BY EDITH WHARTON, 1905

For a thousand years in your sight
   are like yesterday when it is past,
   or like a watch in the night.
. . . .
So teach us to count our days
   that we may gain a wise heart.

PSALM 90:4, 12

Lord of Life, none of us can know the days that remain for us. Teach us to live well, to walk in wisdom through today.

101

—‡— ⁂ —‡—

Speechless before
these budding green spring leaves
in blazing sunlight.

NARROW ROAD TO THE INTERIOR
BY MATSUO BASHŌ, 1694

So if anyone is in Christ, there is a new creation: everything old has passed away; see, everything has become new!

2 CORINTHIANS 5:17

Risen Christ, we rejoice at the newness you bring to the face of the earth and to the barren places in our lives.

A n enormous emotion beat on him; it was like something trying to get in; the pressure of gigantic wings against the glass. Dona nobis pacem. He withstood it, with all the bitter force of the school bench, the cement playground, the St. Pancras waiting-room, Dallow's and Judy's secret lust, and the cold and unhappy moment on the pier. If the glass broke, if the beast—whatever it was—got in, God knows what it would do. He had a sense of huge havoc—the confession, the penance, and the sacrament—an awful distraction, and he drove blind into the rain.

BRIGHTON ROCK BY GRAHAM GREENE, 1938

See that you do not refuse the one who is speaking; for if they did not escape when they refused the one who warned them on earth, how much less will we escape if we reject the one who warns from heaven! . . . Therefore, since we are receiving a kingdom that cannot be shaken, let us give thanks, by which we offer to God an acceptable worship with reverence and awe; for indeed our God is a consuming fire.

HEBREWS 12:25, 28-29

May the peace of God that passes all understanding beat on our hearts—and may we let you in, Great God, to our own great good.

103

Love is holy because it is like grace—the worthiness of its object is never really what matters.

GILEAD BY MARILYNNE ROBINSON, 2004

For the grace of God has appeared, bringing salvation to all, training us to renounce impiety and worldly passions, and in the present age to live lives that are self-controlled, upright, and godly, while we wait for the blessed hope and the manifestation of the glory of our great God and Savior, Jesus Christ.

TITUS 2:11–14

Holy God, we give thanks that imperfect though we may be, you offer us love and grace.

104

What a book the Bible is, what a miracle, what strength is given with it to man. It is like a mold cast of the world and man and human nature, everything is there, and a law for everything for all the ages.

THE BROTHERS KARAMAZOV BY FYODOR DOSTOEVSKY, 1880

I will meditate on your precepts,
   and fix my eyes on your ways.
I will delight in your statutes;
   I will not forget your word.

PSALM 119:15–16

Holy Father, we praise you for your revelation to us in your Scriptures, and in your Word of Life, Christ our Lord.

Why should we be in such desperate haste to succeed, and in such desperate enterprises? If a man does not keep pace with his companions, perhaps it is because he hears a different drummer. Let him step to the music which he hears, however measured or far away.

WALDEN BY HENRY DAVID THOREAU, 1854

For nothing will be impossible with God.

LUKE 1:37

God of dreamers, teach us that your plans for each of us are unique, and that in you what seems impossible is possible.

106

O heart sore-tried! thou hast the best
    That Heaven itself could give thee,—rest,
Rest from all bitter thoughts and things!

FROM *SNOW-BOUND: A WINTER IDYLL*
BY JOHN GREENLEAF WHITTIER, 1866

Why are you cast down, O my soul,
    and why are you disquieted within me?
Hope in God; for I shall again praise him,
    my help and my God.

PSALM 43:5

Holy Father, when our hearts are filled with despair and weariness, we look to you to be our strength and our hope.

107

It was the best of times, it was the worst of times, it was the age of wisdom, it was the age of foolishness, it was the epoch of belief, it was the epoch of incredulity, it was the season of light, it was the season of darkness, it was the spring of hope, it was the winter of despair.

A TALE OF TWO CITIES BY CHARLES DICKENS, 1859

Moreover I saw under the sun that in the place of justice, wickedness was there, and in the place of righteousness, wickedness was there as well. I said in my heart, God will judge the righteous and the wicked, for he has appointed a time for every matter, and for every work.

ECCLESIASTES 3:16–17

Holy Lord, in this world filled with love and hate, with justice and oppression, we remember that you are the Light of the World. Illuminate the darkness, and make yourself known.

108

I am filled with unutterable loathing when I contemplate the religious pomp and show, together with the horrible inconsistencies, which everywhere surround me. . . . The dealers in the bodies of men erect their stand in the presence of the pulpit, and they mutually help each other. The dealer gives his blood-stained gold to support the pulpit, and the pulpit, in return, covers his infernal business with the garb of Christianity. Here we have religion and robbery the allies of each other—devils dressed in angels' robes, and hell presenting the semblance of paradise.

NARRATIVE OF THE LIFE OF FREDERICK DOUGLASS, AN AMERICAN SLAVE BY FREDERICK DOUGLASS, 1845

For the LORD your God is God of gods and Lord of lords, the great God, mighty and awesome, who is not partial and takes no bribe, who executes justice for the orphan and the widow, and who loves the strangers, providing them food and clothing. You shall also love the stranger, for you were strangers in the land of Egypt.

DEUTERONOMY 10:17–19

Lord of all, forgive us for forgetting who we are, for mixing our pursuit of you with human greed and selfish gain.

109

A conscious attempt to fall asleep is sure to produce insomnia, to try to be conscious of one's own digestion is a sure way to upset the stomach. Consciousness is a poison when we apply it to ourselves. Consciousness is a light directed outward. It's like the headlights on a locomotive—turn them inward and you'd have a crash.

DOCTOR ZHIVAGO BY BORIS PASTERNAK, 1957

Do not be conformed to this world, but be transformed by the renewing of your minds, so that you may discern what is the will of God—what is good and acceptable and perfect.

ROMANS 12:2

Lord, guard us against narcissism, and set us free from ways of thinking that blind us to the world around us.

110

Isn't it splendid to think of all the things there are to find out about? It just makes me feel glad to be alive—it's such an interesting world. It wouldn't be half so interesting if we know all about everything, would it? There'd be no scope for imagination then, would there?

ANNE OF GREEN GABLES BY LUCY MAUD MONTGOMERY, 1908

Jesus answered, "Do you believe because I told you that I saw you under the fig tree? You will see greater things than these." And he said to him, "Very truly, I tell you, you will see heaven opened and the angels of God ascending and descending upon the Son of Man."

JOHN 1:50–51

Holy One, awaken our imaginations to the possibilities of your world. May we see your glory reflected in the tiniest creature and in every human heart.

111

The open mind and the receptive heart—which are at last and with fortune's smile the informed mind and the experienced heart—are to be gained anywhere, any time, without necessarily moving an inch from any present address. There must surely be as many ways of seeing a place as there are pairs of eyes to see it.

THE EYE OF THE STORY: SELECTED ESSAYS AND REVIEWS BY EUDORA WELTY, 1978

Open my eyes, so that I may behold
wondrous things out of your law.

PSALM 119:18

Maker of all, give us vision that is alive and attentive, looking for your creative action in the world.

112

-:⸺ ※ ⸺:-

Peace is always beautiful.

FROM *LEAVES OF GRASS*
BY WALT WHITMAN, 1855

> Then justice will dwell in the wilderness,
>   and righteousness abide in the fruitful field.
> The effect of righteousness will be peace,
>   and the result of righteousness, quietness and
>   trust forever.
> My people will abide in a peaceful habitation,
>   in secure dwellings, and in quiet resting places.

ISAIAH 32:16-18

*Prince of Peace, we look with hope to the day when you will
bring peace, healing, and rest to the world.*

113

Our people are good people; our people are kind people. Pray God some day kind people won't all be poor.

THE GRAPES OF WRATH BY JOHN STEINBECK, 1939

Ah, you who make iniquitous decrees,
  who write oppressive statutes,
to turn aside the needy from justice
  and to rob the poor of my people of their right,
that widows may be your spoil,
  and that you may make the orphans your prey!
What will you do on the day of punishment,
  in the calamity that will come from far away?

ISAIAH 10:1–3A

God of all, help us to know truth, to practice justice, and to do kindness to all people.

114

S leep, sleep, old Sun, thou canst not have repast
   As yet, the wound thou took'st on Friday last;
Sleep then, and rest; the world may bear thy stay,
A better Sun rose before thee today,
Who, not content to enlighten all that dwell
On the earth's face, as thou, enlighten'd hell,
And made the dark fires languish in that vale,
As, at thy presence here, our fires grow pale.

FROM "RESURRECTION, IMPERFECT"
BY JOHN DONNE, 1633

As they entered the tomb, they saw a young man, dressed
in a white robe, sitting on the right side; and they were
alarmed. But he said to them, "Do not be alarmed; you are
looking for Jesus of Nazareth, who was crucified. He has
been raised; he is not here. Look, there is the place they
laid him."

MARK 16:5-6

Risen Christ, we praise you, Victor over death, Redeemer of all!

115

The best immortalities—those in the domain of passion—
are still vacant. There is no poet who is the total voice of
love, hate, or despair. That is, the great verses of humanity have
still not been written. This imperfection should raise our hopes.

"LITERARY PLEASURE" BY JORGE LUIS BORGES, 1927

My soul longs, indeed it faints
    for the courts of the LORD;
my heart and my flesh sing for joy
    to the living God.

PSALM 84:2

*O Lord, may we add our voices to the world's songs of
celebration, of lamentation, of anger, and of gratitude, and we
thank you that you delight to hear the longings of our hearts.*

116

In the course of twenty crowded years one parts with many illusions. I did not wish to lose the early ones. Some memories are realities, and are better than anything that can ever happen to one again.

MY ÁNTONIA BY WILLA CATHER, 1918

These things I remember
    as I pour out my soul:
how I went with the throng,
    and led them in procession to the house of God,
with glad shouts and songs of thanksgiving,
    a multitude keeping festival.

PSALM 42:4

Father, when we feel disconnected from our past selves, and when we long for the times when joy felt less muddied by disappointments, we ask that you would carry us and strengthen our burdened hearts.

117

People can learn as much about the ways of God from business deals gone bad or sparrows falling to the ground as they can from reciting the books of the Bible in order. They can learn as much from a love affair or a wildflower as they can from knowing the Ten Commandments by heart.

AN ALTAR IN THE WORLD: A GEOGRAPHY OF FAITH BY BARBARA BROWN TAYLOR, 2009

He also said, "With what can we compare the kingdom of God, or what parable will we use for it? It is like a mustard seed, which, when sown upon the ground, is the smallest of all the seeds on earth; yet when it is sown it grows up and becomes the greatest of all shrubs, and puts forth large branches, so that the birds of the air can make nests in its shade."

With many such parables he spoke the word to them, as they were able to hear it.

MARK 4:30–33

God of Holy Scripture and of the everyday, help us to pay attention to all the ways in which you are moving, all the places where the kingdom is coming near.

118

A thing of beauty is a joy for ever:
　　Its loveliness increases; it will never
Pass into nothingness; but still will keep
A bower quiet for us, and a sleep
Full of sweet dreams, and health, and quiet breathing.

FROM *ENDYMION* BY JOHN KEATS, 1818

How beautiful upon the mountains
　　are the feet of the messenger who announces peace,
who brings good news,
　　who announces salvation,
　　who says to Zion, "Your God reigns."

ISAIAH 52:7

Gracious God, we thank you for drawing us into a place of peace, rest, and shelter.

119

Constantly falling back into an old trap, before I am even fully aware of it, I find myself wondering why someone hurt me, rejected me, or didn't pay attention to me. Without realizing it, I find myself brooding about someone else's success, my own loneliness, and the way the world abuses me. . . . All of these mental games reveal to me the fragility of my faith that I am the Beloved One on whom God's favor rests.

THE RETURN OF THE PRODIGAL SON BY HENRI NOUWEN, 1992

Be still before the LORD, and wait patiently for him;
  do not fret over those who prosper in their way,
  over those who carry out evil devices.

PSALM 37:7

Father, may wrongs done against me not have power over me. Draw me into the freedom of your love.

120

---※---

L ife appears to me too short to be spent in nursing animosity or registering wrongs.

JANE EYRE BY CHARLOTTE BRONTË, 1847

Put away from you all bitterness and wrath and anger and wrangling and slander, together with all malice, and be kind to one another, tenderhearted, forgiving one another, as God in Christ has forgiven you.

EPHESIANS 4:31–32

God who forgives, let your forgiveness take root and grow in our hearts. Free us from the creeping choke of bitterness.

121

L ove is or it ain't. Thin love ain't love at all.

BELOVED BY TONI MORRISON, 1987

Set me as a seal upon your heart,
    as a seal upon your arm;
for love is strong as death.

SONG OF SOLOMON 8:6A

Lord our God, we make our home in your abundant love, and ask that you would make our love like your own.

122

No man, for any considerable period, can wear one face to himself and another to the multitude, without finally getting bewildered as to which may be the true.

THE SCARLET LETTER BY NATHANIEL HAWTHORNE, 1850

See what love the Father has given us, that we should be called children of God; and that is what we are.

1 JOHN 3:1A

Father, it is easy to rifle through various identities, trying to determine which ones we need to put on to be liked, noticed, or admired. Let our identities as your children, as people you love, be the identities we come home to.

123

L et me not to the marriage of true minds
  Admit impediments. Love is not love
Which alters when it alteration finds,
Or bends with the remover to remove.
O no, it is an ever-fixed mark
That looks on tempests and is never shaken.

FROM "LET ME NOT TO THE MARRIAGE
OF TRUE MINDS" (SONNET 116) BY
WILLIAM SHAKESPEARE, 1609

The steadfast love of the LORD never ceases,
    his mercies never come to an end;
they are new every morning;
    great is your faithfulness.

LAMENTATIONS 3:22–23

*Lord our God, in this world where affections can be so fickle
and conditional, we are deeply grateful for your steadfast and
unchanging love.*

124

We walked always in beauty, it seemed to me. We walked and looked about, or stood and looked. Sometimes, less often, we would sit down. We did not often speak. The place spoke for us and was a kind of speech. We spoke to each other in the things we saw.

JAYBER CROW BY WENDELL BERRY, 2000

He loves righteousness and justice;
  the earth is full of the steadfast love of the LORD.
By the word of the LORD the heavens were made,
  and all their host by the breath of his mouth.

PSALM 33:5–6

*Lord of Creation, help us to know you and ourselves in the
beauty you have given us.*

125

⊹—⁑—⊹

I will tell you something about stories,
        [he said]
    They aren't just entertainment.
      Don't be fooled.
    They are all we have, you see,
      all we have to fight off
        illness and death.

CEREMONY BY
LESLIE MARMON SILKO, 1977

All scripture is inspired by God and is useful for teaching, for reproof, for correction, and for training in righteousness, so that everyone who belongs to God may be proficient, equipped for every good work.

2 TIMOTHY 3:16–17

In your word, O Lord, there is wisdom, and in your stories, life.

126

Like winds and sunsets, wild things were taken for granted until progress began to do away with them. Now we face the question whether a still higher "standard of living" is worth its cost in things natural, wild, and free. For us of the minority, the opportunity to see geese is more important than the television, and the chance to find a pasque-flower is a right as inalienable as free speech.

FROM THE FOREWORD TO *A SAND COUNTY ALMANAC* BY ALDO LEOPOLD, 1949

I brought you into a plentiful land
   to eat its fruits and its good things.
But when you entered you defiled my land,
   and made my heritage an abomination.

JEREMIAH 2:7

Holy Lord, forgive us for the ways in which we neglect and transgress your creation, and give us eyes that are attentive to the gift of your world around us.

127

Thinking it would console him, she took a piece of charcoal and erased the innumerable loves that he still owed her for, and she voluntarily brought up her own most solitary sadnesses so as not to leave him alone in his weeping.

ONE HUNDRED YEARS OF SOLITUDE BY
GABRIEL GARCÍA MÁRQUEZ, 1967

Rejoice with those who rejoice, weep with those who weep.

ROMANS 12:15

Lord Christ, you became like us in our sufferings. Give us compassionate solidarity with those around us who walk through sorrow.

128

Yes! Thank God; human feeling is like the mighty rivers that bless the earth: it does not wait for beauty—it flows with resistless force and brings beauty with it.

ADAM BEDE BY GEORGE ELIOT, 1859

I am about to do a new thing;
    now it springs forth, do you not perceive it?
I will make a way in the wilderness
    and rivers in the desert.

ISAIAH 43:19

Our Lord, we thank you for new life, for renewal, for promise, and for tenacious hope.

129

Despair is the price one pays for setting oneself an impossible aim.

THE HEART OF THE MATTER BY GRAHAM GREENE, 1948

Humble yourselves therefore under the mighty hand of God, so that he may exalt you in due time.

1 PETER 5:6

Lord, you know my getting up and my lying down. Help me to do those things you have given me to do, and not to strive needlessly for some vain prize.

130

Must I strive towards colorlessness? But seriously and without snobbery, think of what the world would lose if that should happen. America is woven of many strands. I would recognize them and let it so remain. Our fate is to become one, and yet many.

INVISIBLE MAN BY RALPH ELLISON, 1952

On that day there will be a highway from Egypt to Assyria, and the Assyrian will come into Egypt, and the Egyptian into Assyria, and the Egyptians will worship with the Assyrians.

On that day Israel will be the third with Egypt and Assyria, a blessing in the midst of the earth, whom the LORD of hosts has blessed, saying, "Blessed be Egypt my people, and Assyria the work of my hands, and Israel my heritage."

ISAIAH 19:23–25

Triune God, just as you are one God in three persons, we acknowledge that we are one people made in your image, yet many in our God-given diversity.

131

All the variety, all the charm, all the beauty of life is made up of light and shadow.

ANNA KARENINA BY LEO TOLSTOY, 1877

For everything there is a season, and a time for every
        matter under heaven:
a time to be born, and a time to die;
a time to plant, and a time to pluck up what is planted;
a time to kill, and a time to heal;
a time to break down, and a time to build up;
a time to weep, and a time to laugh;
a time to mourn, and a time to dance.

ECCLESIASTES 3:1-4

God who fashioned the world in all its complexities, open us to the mysteries of this life, and walk us through the ways that are dark to us.

132

And for all this, nature is never spent;
    There lives the dearest freshness deep down things;
And though the last lights off the black West went
    Oh, morning, at the brown brink eastward, springs—
Because the Holy Ghost over the bent
    World broods with warm breast and with ah! bright wings.

FROM "GOD'S GRANDEUR" BY GERARD MANLEY HOPKINS, 1918

O LORD, how manifold are your works!
    In wisdom you have made them all;
    the earth is full of your creatures.

. . . .

When you send forth your spirit, they are created;
    and you renew the face of the ground.

PSALM 104:24, 30

Lord Christ, we remember how you told your followers that it was good for you to leave them, so that the Holy Spirit, the Counselor, would come to abide with them and guide them into the ways of your kingdom. We thank you for this promise!

133

It often happens that two schoolboys can solve difficulties in their work for one another better than the master can. When you took the problem to a master, as we all remember, he was very likely to explain what you understood already, to add a great deal of information which you didn't want, and say nothing at all about the thing that was puzzling you. . . . The fellow-pupil can help more than the master because he knows less. The difficulty we want him to explain is one he has recently met. The expert met it so long ago that he has forgotten.

REFLECTIONS ON THE PSALMS BY C. S. LEWIS, 1958

But God chose what is foolish in the world to shame the wise; God chose what is weak in the world to shame the strong.

1 CORINTHIANS 1:27

God of Wisdom, may we not fear our own lack of understanding, and may we walk with each other through our unknowing.

134

For I have had too much
Of apple-picking: I am overtired
Of the great harvest I myself desired.
There were ten thousand thousand fruit to touch,
Cherish in hand, lift down, and not let fall.
For all
That struck the earth,
No matter if not bruised or spiked with stubble,
Went surely to the cider-apple heap
As of no worth.
One can see what will trouble
This sleep of mine, whatever sleep it is.

FROM "AFTER APPLE-PICKING"
BY ROBERT FROST, 1914

He said, "My presence will go with you, and I will give
you rest."

EXODUS 33:14

*God of Life, when mortality draws near to us more poignantly,
may we find our peace in you, and trust your care over our lives.*

135

‏*❈*‏

People who cannot suffer can never grow up, can never discover who they are.

THE FIRE NEXT TIME BY JAMES BALDWIN, 1963

But he was wounded for our transgressions,
    crushed for our iniquities;
upon him was the punishment that made us whole,
    and by his bruises we are healed.
All we like sheep have gone astray;
    we have all turned to our own way,
and the LORD has laid on him
    the iniquity of us all.

ISAIAH 53:5–6

Dear Christ, you know more than we about suffering. Help us to recognize it as a part of life, to bear it, to learn from it, and to know you accompany us in it.

136

I died for beauty, but was scarce
  Adjusted in the tomb,
When one who died for truth was lain
In an adjoining room.

He questioned softly why I failed?
"For beauty," I replied.
"And I for truth,—Themselves are one;
We brethren are," he said.

And so, as kinsmen, met a night,
We talked between the rooms,
Until the moss had reached our lips,
And covered up our names.

"I DIED FOR BEAUTY" BY
EMILY DICKINSON, 1890

Finally, beloved, whatever is true, whatever is honorable, whatever is just, whatever is pure, whatever is pleasing, whatever is commendable, if there is any excellence and if there is anything worthy of praise, think about these things.

PHILIPPIANS 4:8

Righteous God, make us bearers of truth and beauty in your world.

137

We have done the things we used to plan to do, long ago, when we were Seminarians,—at least some of them. To fulfil the dreams of one's youth; that is the best that can happen to a man. No worldly success can take the place of that.

DEATH COMES FOR THE ARCHBISHOP BY WILLA CATHER, 1927

My soul is satisfied as with a rich feast,
    and my mouth praises you with joyful lips
when I think of you on my bed,
    and meditate on you in the watches of the night.

PSALM 63:5-6

Holy Lord, may we find our satisfaction, our fulfillment, and our joy in you, as we day by day become the people you created us to be.

138

Well-a-well! It's the bad ones as have the broken hearts, sure enough; good folk never get utterly cast down, they've always getten hope in the Lord; it's the sinful as bear the bitter, bitter grief in their crushed hearts, poor souls; it's them we ought, most of all, to pity and to help.

MARY BARTON BY ELIZABETH GASKELL, 1848

The LORD is near to the brokenhearted,
    and saves the crushed in spirit.

PSALM 34:18

Lord, have mercy on me, a sinner, and on all those who fall short of what they should do and where they should be.

139

So little cause for carolings
      Of such ecstatic sound
Was written on terrestrial things
    Afar or nigh around,
That I could think there trembled through
    His happy good-night air
Some blessed Hope, whereof he knew
    And I was unaware.

FROM "THE DARKLING THRUSH"
BY THOMAS HARDY, 1900

But ask the animals, and they will teach you;
    the birds of the air, and they will tell you;
ask the plants of the earth, and they will teach you;
    and the fish of the sea will declare to you.
. . . .
In his hand is the life of every living thing
    and the breath of every human being.

JOB 12:7–8, 10

Lord, may we learn from the singing of the birds and turn our hearts toward gratitude and joy at your presence in the world!

140

---※---

The merciful precepts of Christ will at last suffuse the Code and it will glow with their radiance. Crime will be considered an illness with its own doctors to replace your judges and its hospitals to replace your prisons. Liberty shall be equated with health. Ointments and oil shall be applied to limbs that were once shackled and branded. Infirmities that once were scourged with anger shall now be bathed with love. The cross in place of the gallows: sublime and yet so simple.

THE LAST DAY OF A CONDEMNED MAN BY VICTOR HUGO, 1829

He has abolished the law with its commandments and ordinances, that he might create in himself one new humanity in place of the two, thus making peace, and might reconcile both groups to God in one body through the cross, thus putting to death that hostility through it.

EPHESIANS 2:15–16

Lord Christ, you have turned upside down the old economy.
Draw us into your world of unity and peace.

G ive sorrow words. The grief that does not speak
  Whispers the o'erfraught heart and bids it break.

MACBETH BY WILLIAM SHAKESPEARE, 1606

Cast all your anxiety on him, because he cares for you.

1 PETER 5:7

Loving Father, may we take our fears and sorrows to you, and also to those around us who desire to love us through our trials. Guard us from isolation and despair.

142

In a word, I was too cowardly to do what I knew to be right, as I had been too cowardly to avoid doing what I knew to be wrong.

GREAT EXPECTATIONS BY CHARLES DICKENS, 1860–61

Do not be overcome by evil, but overcome evil with good.

ROMANS 12:21

Holy Father, make us people of courage and bravery, and forgive us for shrinking from the way of truth out of fear or apathy.

143

She has ever listened to the still, small voice within her soul, and followed where it led. She has clothed the naked, and fed the hungry; been bound with those in bondage, and remembered her less fortunate brother when released from chains herself. She has upheld the right and true, denouncing wrong in high places as well as low. Her barque has been carried far out to sea, and now it nears the port. May she encounter no more storms upon her homeward course, but, wafted by soft, sweet winds through placid waters, peacefully enter the harbor of the "King Eternal."

NARRATIVE OF SOJOURNER TRUTH BY SOJOURNER TRUTH, 1850

Therefore, since we are surrounded by so great a cloud of witnesses, let us also lay aside every weight and the sin that clings so closely, and let us run with perseverance the race that is set before us, looking to Jesus the pioneer and perfecter of our faith.

HEBREWS 12:1-2A

Our Lord, we thank you for the brave witness of those who went before us. We know that we are borne along by their prayers, faith, courage, and love.

144

It is perilous to study too deeply the arts of the Enemy, for good or for ill.

THE FELLOWSHIP OF THE RING BY J. R. R. TOLKIEN, 1954

Again, the devil took him to a very high mountain and showed him all the kingdoms of the world and their splendor; and he said to him, "All these I will give you, if you will fall down and worship me." Jesus said to him, "Away with you, Satan! for it is written,

'Worship the Lord your God,
and serve only him.'"

Then the devil left him, and suddenly angels came and waited on him.

MATTHEW 4:8–11

Holy God, keep our eyes on you. Help us follow your path of goodness and forgive us when we stumble.

145

The best preservative to keep the mind in health is the faithful admonition of a friend.

"OF FRIENDSHIP" BY FRANCIS BACON, 1612

Well meant are the wounds a friend inflicts,
   but profuse are the kisses of an enemy.

PROVERBS 27:6

Our Lord, give us the humility to accept correction, to admit that we are wrong, to ask for forgiveness.

146

If they drive God from the earth, we shall shelter Him under ground. One cannot exist in prison without God; it's even more impossible in prison than out. And then we men underground will sing from the bowels of the earth in a glorious hymn to God, with Whom is joy.

THE BROTHERS KARAMAZOV BY FYODOR DOSTOEVSKY, 1880

After they had given [Paul and Silas] a severe flogging, they threw them into prison and ordered the jailer to keep them securely. Following these instructions, he put them in the innermost cell and fastened their feet in the stocks.

About midnight Paul and Silas were praying and singing hymns to God, and the prisoners were listening to them.

ACTS 16:23–25

God of Freedom, we remember those who are in prison. Forgive us for the ways we forget people who are marginalized, and teach us your abundant and seeing love.

When someone dies, you don't get over it by forgetting; you get over it by remembering, and you are aware that no person is ever truly lost or gone once they have been in our life and loved us, as we have loved them.

CEREMONY BY LESLIE MARMON SILKO, 1977

Do not let your hearts be troubled. Believe in God, believe also in me. In my Father's house there are many dwelling places. If it were not so, would I have told you that I go to prepare a place for you? And if I go and prepare a place for you, I will come again and will take you to myself, so that where I am, there you may be also.

JOHN 14:1–3

God of the living and of the dead, remind us that no one is ever truly lost in you.

148

What you're looking for is already inside you. You've heard this before, but the holy thing inside you really is that which causes you to seek it. You can't buy it, lease it, rent it, date it, or apply for it. The best job in the world can't give it to you. Neither can success, or fame, or financial security—besides which, there ain't no such thing.

PLAN B: FURTHER THOUGHTS ON FAITH BY ANNE LAMOTT, 2005

Then Moses summoned Joshua and said to him in the sight of all Israel: "Be strong and bold, for you are the one who will go with this people into the land that the LORD has sworn to their ancestors to give them; and you will put them in possession of it. It is the LORD who goes before you. He will be with you; he will not fail you or forsake you. Do not fear or be dismayed."

DEUTERONOMY 31:7-8

God of Israel, you have given us all we need to do your will. Help us not to be afraid or dismayed, because you go before us.

149

But James, as an artist, was deeply suspicious of what gave him pleasure, or indeed satisfaction. In his own complex sensibility, there was an ambiguity about most things, and this moved him towards a subtlety when he approached character, drama, and scene, and nudged him towards many modifying subclauses when he wrote a sentence. Nothing came to him simply.

THE AMBASSADORS BY HENRY JAMES, 1903

It is the glory of God to conceal things,
    but the glory of kings is to search things out.

PROVERBS 25:2

Lord, your ways are so often complex and indecipherable. Thank you for being big enough for our questions, our searching, and our doubt.

150

Silence is the best response to mystery.

DAKOTA: A SPIRITUAL GEOGRAPHY
BY KATHLEEN NORRIS, 1993

The LORD is good to those who wait for him,
   to the soul that seeks him.
It is good that one should wait quietly
   for the salvation of the LORD.

LAMENTATIONS 3:25–26

Lord of earth and sky, help me to find a time and place to contemplate your wonders in silence, and to know your still, small voice.

151

Perhaps we all lose our sense of reality to the precise degree to which we are engrossed in our own work, and perhaps that is why we see in the increasing complexity of our mental constructs a means for greater understanding, even while intuitively we know that we shall never be able to fathom the imponderables that govern our course through life.

THE RINGS OF SATURN BY W. G. SEBALD, 1995

For there is still a vision for the appointed time;
    it speaks of the end, and does not lie.
If it seems to tarry, wait for it;
    it will surely come, it will not delay.

HABAKKUK 2:3

Lord God, in the face of all we can't understand, grant us the trust to rely on your wisdom and the patience to wait for your promises.

152

One day I'll own my own house, but I won't forget who I am or where I came from. Passing bums will ask, Can I come in? I'll offer them the attic, ask them to stay, because I know how it is to be without a house.

THE HOUSE ON MANGO STREET BY SANDRA CISNEROS, 1984

Is not this the fast that I choose:
    to loose the bonds of injustice,
    to undo the thongs of the yoke,
to let the oppressed go free,
    and to break every yoke?
Is it not to share your bread with the hungry,
    and bring the homeless poor into your house;
when you see the naked, to cover them,
    and not to hide yourself from your own kin?

ISAIAH 58:6–7

Grant, O Lord, that we might share our bread with the hungry and offer the homeless a shelter from the storm, for every child of God is of our own kin.

153

I will honour Christmas in my heart, and try to keep it all the year. I will live in the Past, the Present, and the Future. The Spirits of all Three shall strive within me. I will not shut out the lessons that they teach.

A CHRISTMAS CAROL BY CHARLES DICKENS, 1843

So they went with haste and found Mary and Joseph, and the child lying in the manger. When they saw this, they made known what had been told them about this child; and all who heard it were amazed at what the shepherds told them. But Mary treasured all these words and pondered them in her heart.

LUKE 2:16-19

Lord Christ, may our hearts be like Mary's, taking within us your words and allowing them to take root, to grow, and to bear fruit.

154

M an can do anything if he wishes to enough, St. Peter believed. Desire is creation, is the magical element in that process. If there were an instrument by which to measure desire, one could foretell achievement.

THE PROFESSOR'S HOUSE BY WILLA CATHER, 1925

Trust in him at all times, O people;
  pour out your heart before him;
  God is a refuge for us.

PSALM 62:8

Lord, you know the desires of our hearts. Fulfill them, as may be best for us.

155

There is nothing I would not do for those who are really my friends. I have no notion of loving people by halves, it is not my nature.

NORTHANGER ABBEY BY JANE AUSTEN, 1818

This is my commandment, that you love one another as I have loved you. No one has greater love than this, to lay down one's life for one's friends.

JOHN 15:12–13

Lord Christ, give us the strength and courage to love with all our hearts.

"The cross cannot be defeated," said MacIan, "for it is Defeat."

THE BALL AND THE CROSS BY G. K. CHESTERTON, 1909

He himself bore our sins in his body on the cross, so that, free from sins, we might live for righteousness; by his wounds you have been healed.

1 PETER 2:24

Our Lord Christ, we are continually filled with awe at the gift of your life, given for us.

157

M eg, when people don't know who they are, they are open either to being Xed, or Named.

A WIND IN THE DOOR BY MADELEINE L'ENGLE, 1973

Discipline yourselves, keep alert. Like a roaring lion your adversary the devil prowls around, looking for someone to devour. Resist him, steadfast in your faith, for you know that your brothers and sisters in all the world are undergoing the same kinds of suffering.

1 PETER 5:8–9

O Lord, you know us and name us and claim us. Help us to know who you are and to what you have called us, that we may live into our names as your faithful children.

158

I stood on ground of holiness and bowed;
 The River Jordan flowed past my feet
As the angel soothed my soul with song,
A song of wonderful sweetness.
I stooped and washed my soul in Jordan's stream
Ere my Redeemer came to take me home;
I stooped and washed my soul in waters pure
As the breathing of a new-born child

FROM "A DREAM" (THE FIRST OF
THE "TWO NEGRO SPIRITUALS")
BY FENTON JOHNSON, 1921

How precious is your steadfast love, O God!
  All people may take refuge in the shadow of your wings.
They feast on the abundance of your house,
  and you give them drink from the river of your delights.
For with you is the fountain of life;
  in your light we see light.

PSALM 36:7-9

*O Lord, we thank you for your living water that renews us day
by day.*

159

It is difficult to undo our own damage, and to recall to our presence that which we have asked to leave. It is hard to desecrate a grove and change your mind. The very holy mountains are keeping mum. We doused the burning bush and cannot rekindle it. . . . It could be that wherever there is motion there is noise, as when a whale breaches and smacks the water—and wherever there is stillness there is the still small voice, God's speaking from the whirlwind, nature's old song and dance, the show we drove from town.

TEACHING A STONE TO TALK BY ANNIE DILLARD, 1982

He said, "Go out and stand on the mountain before the LORD, for the LORD is about to pass by." Now there was a great wind, so strong that it was splitting mountains and breaking rocks in pieces before the LORD, but the LORD was not in the wind; and after the wind an earthquake, but the LORD was not in the earthquake; and after the earthquake a fire, but the LORD was not in the fire; and after the fire a sound of sheer silence. When Elijah heard it, he wrapped his face in his mantle and went out and stood at the entrance of the cave. Then there came a voice to him that said, "What are you doing here, Elijah?"

1 KINGS 19:11–13

God who speaks, give us ears that listen for your voice. Teach us to quiet the world around us, so that we can hear you.

160

·⊹—⁂—⊹·

V isit then this soul of mine,
  Pierce the gloom of sin and grief;
Fill me, Radiancy Divine!
Scatter all my unbelief:
More and more thyself display,
Shining to the perfect day!

FROM "MORNING HYMN"
BY CHARLES WESLEY, 1740

Be merciful to me, O God, be merciful to me,
    for in you my soul takes refuge;
in the shadow of your wings I will take refuge,
    until the destroying storms pass by.
I cry to God Most High,
    to God who fulfills his purpose for me.

PSALM 57:1–2

Lord of Light, we look to you to heal us, to preserve us, to carry us.

161

We live on a little island of the articulable, which we tend to mistake for reality itself. We can and do make small and tedious lives as we sail through the cosmos on our uncannily lovely little planet, and this is surely remarkable. But we do so much else besides. For example, we make language. A language is a grand collaboration, a collective art form which we begin to master as babes and sucklings, and which we preserve, modify, cull, enlarge as we pass through our lives.

"IMAGINATION AND COMMUNITY"
BY MARILYNNE ROBINSON, 2012

I will give thanks to the LORD with my whole heart;
    I will tell of all your wonderful deeds.
I will be glad and exult in you;
    I will sing praise to your name, O Most High.

PSALM 9:1–2

Holy Lord, we thank you for the gift of language, whether in writing, song, or conversation, which we can lift to you in praise and gratitude!

162

Silence is the perfectest herald of joy. I were but little happy if I could say how much.

MUCH ADO ABOUT NOTHING BY WILLIAM SHAKESPEARE, 1612

When they saw that the star had stopped, they were overwhelmed with joy. On entering the house, they saw the child with Mary his mother; and they knelt down and paid him homage. Then, opening their treasure chests, they offered him gifts of gold, frankincense, and myrrh.

MATTHEW 2:10-11

Holy One, let us know your joy, and accept our gratitude for all your good gifts, especially Christ our Lord.

163

I know what the caged bird feels, alas!
　　When the sun is bright on the upland slopes;
When the wind stirs soft through the springing grass,
And the river flows like a stream of glass;
　　When the first bird sings and the first bud opes,
And the faint perfume from its chalice steals—
I know what the caged bird feels!

FROM "SYMPATHY"
BY PAUL LAURENCE DUNBAR, 1893

O LORD, how long shall I cry for help,
　　and you will not listen?
Or cry to you "Violence!"
　　and you will not save?

HABAKKUK 1:2

O Christ who came to set us free, we call out to you for justice for the oppressed, for salvation and renewal for those in sorrow.

164

-:-— ✳ ——:-

It is because good is always stronger than evil. Always remember that, Antonio. The smallest bit of good can stand against all the powers of evil in the world and it will emerge triumphant.

BLESS ME, ULTIMA BY RUDOLFO ANAYA, 1972

Do not repay evil for evil or abuse for abuse; but, on the contrary, repay with a blessing. It is for this that you were called—that you might inherit a blessing.

1 PETER 3:9

Great Source of all that is good and beautiful, help us to light up the darkness, to be your agents of goodness in the world.

165

Celebration belongs to God's Kingdom. God not only offers forgiveness, reconciliation, and healing, but wants to lift up these gifts as a source of joy for all who witness them.

THE RETURN OF THE PRODIGAL SON BY HENRI NOUWEN, 1992

> Ho, everyone who thirsts,
>   come to the waters;
> and you that have no money,
>   come, buy and eat!
> Come, buy wine and milk
>   without money and without price.

ISAIAH 55:1

We praise you, O God, that your kingdom is one of abundance and joy, filled with the celebration of new life!

166

S he could not explain in so many words, but she felt that those who prepare for all the emergencies of life beforehand may equip themselves at the expense of joy.

HOWARD'S END BY E. M. FORSTER, 1910

So do not worry about tomorrow, for tomorrow will bring worries of its own. Today's trouble is enough for today.

MATTHEW 6:34

Lord Christ, so many times in the Scriptures you told your followers not to worry. May we not waste our days trying to protect ourselves from problems dreamed up by our minds; give us the trust to live in today.

167

We are cruelly trapped between what we would like to be and what we actually are. And we cannot possibly become what we would like to be until we are willing to ask ourselves just why the lives we lead on this continent are mainly so empty, so tame, and so ugly.

I AM NOT YOUR NEGRO BY JAMES BALDWIN, 2017

I do not understand my own actions. For I do not do what I want, but I do the very thing I hate. Now if I do what I do not want, I agree that the law is good. But in fact it is no longer I that do it, but sin that dwells within me. For I know that nothing good dwells within me, that is, in my flesh. I can will what is right, but I cannot do it. For I do not do the good I want, but the evil I do not want is what I do. Now if I do what I do not want, it is no longer I that do it, but sin that dwells within me.

ROMANS 7:15-20

Lord, we repent of our sin—personal, social, and institutional—and we crave your forgiveness and the strength to move forward into what we would like to be, what you would have us be.

168

The secret of the Great Stories is that they *have* no secrets. The Great Stories are the ones you have heard and want to hear again. . . . You know how they end, yet you listen as though you don't. In the way that although you know that one day you will die, you live as though you won't. In the Great Stories you know who lives, who dies, who finds love, who doesn't. And yet you want to know again.

THE GOD OF SMALL THINGS BY ARUNDHATI ROY, 1997

The spirit of the Lord God is upon me,
    because the Lord has anointed me;
he has sent me to bring good news to the oppressed,
    to bind up the brokenhearted,
to proclaim liberty to the captives,
    and release to the prisoners.

ISAIAH 61:1

Lord Christ, we thank you for yours, the best of stories, that was told even before your birth and that continues to make itself new to us.

169

‑•‑——— ※ ———‑•‑

A wonderful fact to reflect upon, that every human creature is constituted to be that profound secret and mystery to every other.

A TALE OF TWO CITIES BY CHARLES DICKENS, 1859

For what human being knows what is truly human except the human spirit that is within? So also no one comprehends what is truly God's except the Spirit of God.

1 CORINTHIANS 2:11

Our Father, however unknown we are to each other, or even to ourselves, we thank you for the comfort and hope of the promise that to you, each of us is fully known.

170

I swear I think there is nothing but immortality!
  That the exquisite scheme is for it, and the nebulous
    float is for it,
  and the cohering is for it,
And all preparation is for it . . . and identity is for it . . .
    and life and
  death are for it.

FROM *LEAVES OF GRASS* BY WALT WHITMAN, 1855

He is the image of the invisible God, the firstborn of all
creation; for in him all things in heaven and on earth were
created, things visible and invisible, whether thrones or
dominions or rulers or powers—all things have been created through him and for him. He himself is before all
things, and in him all things hold together. He is the head
of the body, the church; he is the beginning, the firstborn
from the dead, so that he might come to have first place
in everything.

COLOSSIANS 1:15–18

*Risen Lord, we praise you for being the Source of life, the Victor
over death, and the Author of our faith!*

171

People glorify all sorts of bravery except the bravery they might show on behalf of their nearest neighbors.

MIDDLEMARCH BY GEORGE ELIOT, 1871–72

> He said to him, "'You shall love the Lord your God with all your heart, and with all your soul, and with all your mind.' This is the greatest and first commandment. And a second is like it: 'You shall love your neighbor as yourself.' On these two commandments hang all the law and the prophets."

MATTHEW 22:37–40

Our Father, it can be easy to be blind to the needs closest to us. May our virtue not live in glorified visions of how we might meet faraway needs, but in the simple, necessary flesh and blood of the relationships of our lives.

172

The blue sky is the temple's arch,
Its transept earth and air,
The music of its starry march
The chorus of a prayer.

So Nature keeps the reverent frame
With which her years began,
And all her signs and voices shame
The prayerless heart of man.

FROM "THE WORSHIP OF NATURE"
BY JOHN GREENLEAF WHITTIER, 1857

For what can be known about God is plain to them, because God has shown it to them. Ever since the creation of the world his eternal power and divine nature, invisible though they are, have been understood and seen through the things he has made.

ROMANS 1:19–20A

O Lord, let us join the world around us in proclaiming your glory, and fill our hearts with celebration of your goodness!

L oyalty and obedience to wisdom and justice are fine; but it is still finer to defy arbitrary power, unjustly and cruelly used—not on behalf of ourselves, but on behalf of others more helpless.

NORTH AND SOUTH BY ELIZABETH GASKELL, 1854-55

Then you shall call, and the LORD will answer;
    you shall cry for help, and he will say, Here I am.
If you remove the yoke from among you,
    the pointing of the finger, the speaking of evil,
if you offer your food to the hungry
    and satisfy the needs of the afflicted,
then your light shall rise in the darkness
    and your gloom be like the noonday.

ISAIAH 58:9-10

God who sees the stranger, may our voices and actions work for the cause of justice for the oppressed. Give us attentiveness to the powers we have, and may we use them well.

174

I must say a word about fear. It is life's only true opponent. Only fear can defeat life. It is a clever, treacherous adversary, how well I know. It has no decency, respects no law or convention, shows no mercy. It goes for your weakest spot, which it finds with unnerving ease. It begins in your mind, always . . . so you must fight hard to express it. You must fight hard to shine the light of words upon it. Because if you don't, if your fear becomes a wordless darkness that you avoid, perhaps even manage to forget, you open yourself to further attacks of fear because you never truly fought the opponent who defeated you.

LIFE OF PI BY YANN MARTEL, 2001

While he was still speaking, some people came from the leader's house to say, "Your daughter is dead. Why trouble the teacher any further?" But overhearing what they said, Jesus said to the leader of the synagogue, "Do not fear, only believe."

MARK 5:35–36

Jesus, may we know your peace, and may our fear vanish in the light of your holy presence.

175

"What is a secret wish?"
"It is what you want but cannot ask."

THE JOY LUCK CLUB BY AMY TAN, 1989

I did not speak in secret,
    in a land of darkness;
I did not say to the offspring of Jacob,
    "Seek me in chaos."
I the Lord speak the truth,
    I declare what is right.

ISAIAH 45:19

O God, you know us and all our secrets. Give us the things we need but dare not ask for, and make us secure in your steadfast love.

176

I think it's God that makes people care for people, Jefferson. I think it's God makes children play and people sing. I believe it's God that brings loved ones together. I believe it's God that makes trees bud and food grow out of the earth.

A LESSON BEFORE DYING BY ERNEST GAINES, 1993

The LORD passed before him, and proclaimed,
"The LORD, the LORD,
a God merciful and gracious,
slow to anger,
and abounding in steadfast love and faithfulness,
keeping steadfast love for the thousandth generation,
forgiving iniquity and transgression and sin."

EXODUS 34:6–7A

Gracious God, we give thanks for this world, for this life, for those we love, and for those who love us. Thank you.

And so it happened again, the daily miracle whereby interiority opens out and brings to bloom the million-petalled flower of being here, in the world, with other people. Neither as hard as she had thought it might be nor as easy as it appeared.

ON BEAUTY BY ZADIE SMITH, 2005

Above all, maintain constant love for one another, for love covers a multitude of sins.

1 PETER 4:8

Triune God, origin of fellowship and love, we thank you for the gift of other people. May we see them and let them see us.

178

When you visualized a man or woman carefully, you could always begin to feel pity . . . that was a quality God's image carried with it . . . when you saw the lines at the corners of the eyes, the shape of the mouth, how the hair grew, it was impossible to hate. Hate was just a failure of imagination.

THE POWER AND THE GLORY BY GRAHAM GREENE, 1940

And all of us, with unveiled faces, seeing the glory of the Lord as though reflected in a mirror, are being transformed into the same image from one degree of glory to another; for this comes from the Lord, the Spirit.

2 CORINTHIANS 3:18

Maker of all, help us to be attentive to your image in the lives of those around us, and may we honor that image.

If nature has made you for a giver, your hands are born open, and so is your heart; and though there may be times when your hands are empty, your heart is always full, and you can give things out of that—warm things, kind things, sweet things—help and comfort and laughter—and sometimes gay, kind laughter is the best help of all.

A LITTLE PRINCESS BY FRANCES HODGSON BURNETT, 1905

A cheerful heart is a good medicine,
but a downcast spirit dries up the bones.

PROVERBS 17:22

Holy Lord, we remember how you gave Isaac, the child of promise, the name of Laughter. We thank you that you are a God of humor, celebration, and deep joy.

180

As the pain that can be told is but half a pain, so the pity that questions has little healing in its touch. What Lily craved was the darkness made by enfolding arms, the silence which is not solitude, but compassion holding its breath.

THE HOUSE OF MIRTH BY EDITH WHARTON, 1905

The LORD will fight for you, and you have only to keep still.

EXODUS 14:14

Lord God, make us better listeners. May we not diminish the troubles of our friends and loved ones out of our own discomfort with sitting in suffering. May all of us keep still, and rely on you to fight for us.

181

Oh, how one wishes sometimes to escape from the meaningless dullness of human eloquence, from all those sublime phrases, to take refuge in nature, apparently so inarticulate, or in the wordlessness of long, grinding labor, of sound sleep, of true music, or of a human understanding rendered speechless by emotion.

DOCTOR ZHIVAGO BY BORIS PASTERNAK, 1957

Where were you when I laid the foundation of the earth?
    Tell me, if you have understanding.
. . . .
Have you commanded the morning since your days began,
    and caused the dawn to know its place,
so that it might take hold of the skirts of the earth,
    and the wicked be shaken out of it?

JOB 38:4, 12–13

Lord, just as Job's friends did not bring him good counsel, we recognize that we may also be more harmful than helpful to those around us. Make us attentive to the true needs of others, and thank you for making your voice known, despite our weakness.

182

-:———— ☀ ————:-

What is the nature of the search? you ask. The search is what anyone would undertake if he were not sunk in the everydayness of his own life. To become aware of the search is to be onto something. Not to be onto something is to be in despair.

THE MOVIEGOER BY WALKER PERCY, 1961

So teach us to count our days
   that we may gain a wise heart.

PSALM 90:12

Eternal God, help us to make the most of the days you have given us, to love extravagantly, to gain a heart of wisdom.

183

O Attic shape! Fair attitude! With brede
   Of marble men and maidens overwrought,
With forest branches and the trodden weed;
   Thou, silent form, dost tease us out of thought
As doth eternity: Cold Pastoral!
   When old age shall this generation waste,
      Thou shalt remain, in midst of other woe
Than ours, a friend to man, to whom thou say'st,
   "Beauty is truth, truth beauty,—that is all
   Ye know on earth, and all ye need to know."

FROM "ODE ON A GRECIAN URN"
BY JOHN KEATS, 1820

The grass withers, the flower fades,
   when the breath of the LORD blows upon it;
   surely the people are grass.
The grass withers, the flower fades;
   but the word of our God will stand forever.

ISAIAH 40:7–8

Lord Christ, you are the Eternal Word, the True Vine who abides forever.

184

There is no hopelessness so sad as that of early youth, when the soul is made up of wants, and has no long memories, no super-added life in the life of others; though we who look on think lightly of such premature despair, as if our vision of the future lightened the blind sufferer's present.

THE MILL ON THE FLOSS BY GEORGE ELIOT, 1860

Do not let those who hope in you be put to shame
        because of me,
    O Lord GOD of hosts,
do not let those who seek you be dishonored
        because of me,
    O God of Israel.

PSALM 69:6

Lord Christ, may we be always respectful and honoring of the longings and sufferings in the hearts of others. Fill us with your compassion.

185

I am beginning now to see how radically the character of my spiritual journey will change when I no longer think of God as hiding out and making it as difficult as possible for me to find him, but, instead, as the one who is looking for me while I am doing the hiding.

THE RETURN OF THE PRODIGAL SON BY HENRI NOUWEN, 1992

Which one of you, having a hundred sheep and losing one of them, does not leave the ninety-nine in the wilderness and go after the one that is lost until he finds it? When he has found it, he lays it on his shoulders and rejoices. . . . Just so, I tell you, there will be more joy in heaven over one sinner who repents than over ninety-nine righteous persons who need no repentance.

LUKE 15:4–5, 7

Our Loving Father, we thank you that you pursue us with your fierce and tender love, even when we hide ourselves out of shame, insecurity, or fear.

186

Was it by reason that I attained to the knowledge that I must love my neighbour and not throttle him? . . . Reason has discovered the struggle for existence and the law that I must throttle all those who hinder the satisfaction of my desires. That is the deduction reason makes. But the law of loving others could not be discovered by reason, because it is unreasonable.

ANNA KARENINA BY LEO TOLSTOY, 1877

But I say to you, Love your enemies and pray for those who persecute you, so that you may be children of your Father in heaven; for he makes his sun rise on the evil and on the good, and sends rain on the righteous and on the unrighteous.

MATTHEW 5:44–45

O Christ, the command to love our enemies is a hard one. Fill us with the knowledge of your love and forgiveness for us, that we might extend that love and forgiveness to others.

187

"This is to assuage our conscience, darling," she would explain to Blanca. "But it doesn't help the poor. They don't need charity; they need justice."

THE HOUSE OF THE SPIRITS BY ISABEL ALLENDE, 1982

Even though you offer me your burnt offerings and grain
    offerings,
  I will not accept them;
and the offerings of well-being of your fatted animals
  I will not look upon.
Take away from me the noise of your songs;
  I will not listen to the melody of your harps.
But let justice roll down like waters,
  and righteousness like an ever-flowing stream.

AMOS 5:22–24

Holy One, make us fountains of justice and streams of righteousness, that your grace might flow through us and into the world.

188

We have such numerous interests in our lives that it is not uncommon, on a single occasion, for the foundations of a happiness that does not yet exist to be laid down alongside the intensification of a grief from which we are still suffering.

SWANN'S WAY BY MARCEL PROUST, 1913

Sing praises to the LORD, O you his faithful ones,
   and give thanks to his holy name.
For his anger is but for a moment;
   his favor is for a lifetime.
Weeping may linger for the night,
   but joy comes with the morning.

PSALM 30:4-5

Lord of all, we thank you that you know all of our griefs, and we look with expectation for the return of joy.

189

M y bounty is as boundless as the sea,
My love as deep; the more I give to thee,
The more I have, for both are infinite.

ROMEO AND JULIET BY
WILLIAM SHAKESPEARE, 1597

May the Lord direct your hearts to the love of God and to
the steadfastness of Christ.

2 THESSALONIANS 3:5

*Help us, Triune God, to love as you love: eternal and infinite, a
love as boundless as the sea.*

190

It was only by following the course time prescribed that we could hasten through the gigantic spaces separating us from each other.

AUSTERLITZ BY W. G. SEBALD, 2001

As God's chosen ones, holy and beloved, clothe yourselves with compassion, kindness, humility, meekness, and patience. Bear with one another and, if anyone has a complaint against another, forgive each other; just as the Lord has forgiven you, so you also must forgive.

COLOSSIANS 3:12–13

Loving God, reveal to us the chasms between ourselves and others and give us the courage to bridge the divide.

191

Once the storm is over you won't remember how you made it through, how you managed to survive. You won't even be sure, in fact, whether the storm is really over. But one thing is certain. When you come out of the storm you won't be the same person who walked in.

KAFKA ON THE SHORE BY HARUKI MURAKAMI, 2002

Come to me, all you that are weary and carrying heavy burdens, and I will give you rest. Take my yoke upon you, and learn from me; for I am gentle and humble in heart, and you will find rest for your souls. For my yoke is easy, and my burden is light.

MATTHEW 11:28-30

Lord God, we give thanks that you accompany us through every storm and in every journey, and that you seek for us more than we could ever seek for ourselves.

192

"Help" is a prayer that is always answered. It doesn't matter how you pray—with your head bowed in silence, or crying out in grief, or dancing. Churches are good for prayer, but so are garages and cars and mountains and showers and dance floors. Years ago I wrote an essay that began, "Some people think that God is in the details, but I have come to believe that God is in the bathroom."

PLAN B: FURTHER THOUGHTS ON FAITH BY ANNE LAMOTT, 2005

Those who love me, I will deliver;
   I will protect those who know my name.
When they call to me, I will answer them;
   I will be with them in trouble,
   I will rescue them and honor them.
With long life I will satisfy them,
   and show them my salvation.

PSALM 91:14-16

Help us, O Lord. Deliver us from our troubles, rescue us and protect us, for we trust in your steadfast love.

193

B ut when a man suspects any wrong, it sometimes happens that if he be already involved in the matter, he insensibly strives to cover up his suspicions even from himself. And much this way it was with me. I said nothing, and tried to think nothing.

MOBY-DICK BY HERMAN MELVILLE, 1851

No one who conceals transgressions will prosper,
    but one who confesses and forsakes them
        will obtain mercy.

PROVERBS 28:13

Lord God, give us the courage to confess our sins, to admit our wrongs, and to trust in your forgiveness.

194

That is not to suggest that we can live harmlessly, or strictly at our own expense; we depend upon other creatures and survive by their deaths. To live, we must daily break the body and shed the blood of Creation. When we do this knowingly, lovingly, skillfully, reverently, it is a sacrament. When we do it ignorantly, greedily, clumsily, destructively, it is a desecration.

"THE GIFT OF GOOD LAND" BY WENDELL BERRY, 1981

The land shall not be sold in perpetuity, for the land is mine; with me you are but aliens and tenants. Throughout the land that you hold, you shall provide for the redemption of the land.

LEVITICUS 25:23–24

Holy Lord, as we live, work, and love on this earth you have made, may we do all things with care and gratitude, acknowledging the holiness of the ground we walk upon.

195

We know that God is everywhere; but certainly we feel His presence most when His works are on the grandest scale spread before us; and it is in the unclouded night-sky, where His worlds wheel their silent course, that we read clearest His infinitude, His omnipotence, His omnipresence.

JANE EYRE BY CHARLOTTE BRONTË, 1847

Ah Lord GOD! It is you who made the heavens and the earth by your great power and by your outstretched arm! Nothing is too hard for you.

JEREMIAH 32:17

Lord God, who flung the skies and stretched the seas, help us to know your presence, and to offer praise for your magnificence.

196

With his fabulous tale to proclaim, the preacher is called in his turn to stand up in his pulpit as fabulist extraordinary, to tell the truth of the Gospel in its highest and wildest and holiest sense. This is his job, but more often than not he shrinks from it because the truth he is called to proclaim, like the fairy tale, seems in all but some kind of wistful, faraway sense too good to be true, and so the preacher as apologist instead of fabulist tries as best as he can to pare it down to a size he thinks the world will swallow.

TELLING THE TRUTH: THE GOSPEL AS TRAGEDY, COMEDY, AND FAIRY TALE BY FREDERICK BUECHNER, 1977

Where is the one who is wise? Where is the scribe? Where is the debater of this age? Has not God made foolish the wisdom of the world? For since, in the wisdom of God, the world did not know God through wisdom, God decided, through the foolishness of our proclamation, to save those who believe.

1 CORINTHIANS 1:20–21

Lord God, may we not try to diminish you to make you more comprehensible, but instead let us accept the wild and foolish abundance of your story of love and redemption.

197

You were made for enjoyment, and the world was filled with things which you will enjoy, unless you are too proud to be pleased with them, or too grasping to care for what you cannot turn to other account than mere delight. Remember that the most beautiful things in the world are the most useless: peacocks and lilies, for instance.

THE STONES OF VENICE BY JOHN RUSKIN, 1853

You prepare a table before me
    in the presence of my enemies;
you anoint my head with oil;
    my cup overflows.

PSALM 23:5

Lord Christ, whose first miracle was to make water into wine, we thank you that you are a God of abundance, beauty, delight, and generosity.

198

I have observed this in my experience of slavery,—that whenever my condition was improved, instead of its increasing my contentment, it only increased my desire to be free, and set me to thinking of plans to gain my freedom. I have found that, to make a contented slave, it is necessary to make a thoughtless one . . . he must be made to feel that slavery is right; and he can be brought to that only when he ceases to be a man.

NARRATIVE OF THE LIFE OF FREDERICK DOUGLASS, AN AMERICAN SLAVE BY FREDERICK DOUGLASS, 1845

Now the Lord is the Spirit, and where the Spirit of the Lord is, there is freedom.

2 CORINTHIANS 3:17

Lord Christ, bring deep and lasting freedom to places of oppression and evil, and may your Spirit of Peace abide with us.

L ook at everything always as though you were seeing it either for the first or last time: Thus is your time on earth filled with glory.

A TREE GROWS IN BROOKLYN BY BETTY SMITH, 1943

For everything created by God is good, and nothing is to be rejected, provided it is received with thanksgiving.

1 TIMOTHY 4:4

God, you sustain the earth with your breath. Give us eyes to see the daily miracles around us.

200

M e and you, we got more yesterday than anybody. We need some kind of tomorrow.

BELOVED BY TONI MORRISON, 1987

Call to me and I will answer you, and will tell you great and hidden things that you have not known.

JEREMIAH 33:3

Lord our God, we look to you in hope, and ask that you bring us healing and renewal.

201

When you love you wish to do things for. You wish to sacrifice for. You wish to serve.

A FAREWELL TO ARMS BY ERNEST HEMINGWAY, 1929

Let love be genuine; hate what is evil, hold fast to what is good; love one another with mutual affection; outdo one another in showing honor.

ROMANS 12:9–10

Help us, Lord, to set aside our selfishness and live for each other, to love sacrificially.

202

I think there's just one kind of folks. Folks.

TO KILL A MOCKINGBIRD
BY HARPER LEE, 1960

You shall not take vengeance or bear a grudge against any
of your people, but you shall love your neighbor as yourself: I am the LORD.

   . . . The alien who resides with you shall be to you as
the citizen among you; you shall love the alien as yourself,
for you were aliens in the land of Egypt: I am the LORD
your God.

LEVITICUS 19:18, 34

God our Father, fill our hearts with love for all people, made in
your image and kept in life by your Word of Life.

203

There is an indifferent, or even negative, attitude toward silence which sees in it a disparagement of God's revelation in the Word. This is the view which misinterprets silence as a ceremonial gesture, as a mystical desire to get beyond the Word. This is to miss the essential relationship of silence to the Word. . . .

Silence is nothing else but waiting for God's Word and coming from God's Word with a blessing. But everybody knows that this is something that needs to be practiced and learned, in these days when talkativeness prevails.

LIFE TOGETHER BY DIETRICH BONHOEFFER, 1939

For God alone my soul waits in silence;
from him comes my salvation.

PSALM 62:1

God who speaks to us, give us the willingness to be silent so we might listen to and follow your Word.

204

-†————※————†-

Until the day when God shall deign to reveal the future to man, all human wisdom is summed up in these two words, —Wait and Hope.

THE COUNT OF MONTE CRISTO BY ALEXANDRE DUMAS, 1844-45

I wait for the LORD, my soul waits,
    and in his word I hope;
my soul waits for the Lord
    more than those who watch for the morning,
    more than those who watch for the morning.

PSALM 130:5-6

Lord our God, in the face of so many things beyond our comprehension, we look to you to be our hope, our wisdom in the midst of all that is unknown.

205

Although there was always generosity in the Negro neighborhood, it was indulged on pain of sacrifice. Whatever was given by Black people to other Blacks was most probably needed as desperately by the donor as by the receiver. A fact which made the giving or receiving a rich exchange.

I KNOW WHY THE CAGED BIRD SINGS BY MAYA ANGELOU, 1969

And in this matter I am giving my advice: it is appropriate for you who began last year not only to do something but even to desire to do something—now finish doing it, so that your eagerness may be matched by completing it according to your means. For if the eagerness is there, the gift is acceptable according to what one has—not according to what one does not have.

2 CORINTHIANS 8:10–12

Generous God, help us to fearlessly give to others from those things that you have given us.

206

Wonderfullest things are ever the unmentionable; deep memories yield no epitaphs.

MOBY-DICK BY HERMAN MELVILLE, 1851

O the depth of the riches and wisdom and knowledge of God! How unsearchable are his judgments and how inscrutable his ways!

ROMANS 11:33

Holy God, you know all that lies unspoken or hidden within our deepest selves. We praise you for knowing us more fully than we know ourselves.

M y heart was heavy, for its trust had been
   Abused, its kindness answered with foul wrong;
So, turning gloomily from my fellow-men,
One summer Sabbath day I strolled among
The green mounds of the village burial-place;
Where, pondering how all human love and hate
Find one sad level; and how, soon or late,
Wronged and wrongdoer, each with meekened face,
And cold hands folded over a still heart,
Pass the green threshold of our common grave,
Whither all footsteps tend, whence none depart,
Awed for myself, and pitying my race,
Our common sorrow, like a mighty wave,
Swept all my pride away, and trembling I forgave!

"FORGIVENESS" BY JOHN GREENLEAF WHITTIER, 1857

One who forgives an affront fosters friendship,
   but one who dwells on disputes will alienate a friend.

PROVERBS 17:9

Holy God, set us free from choking bitterness, and fill our hearts with forgiveness.

208

At a distance from facts one draws conclusions which appear infallible, which yet when put to the test of reality, vanish like unreal dreams.

THE LAST MAN BY MARY SHELLEY, 1826

The simple believe everything,
  but the clever consider their steps.
The wise are cautious and turn away from evil,
  but the fool throws off restraint and is careless.

PROVERBS 14:15–16

Our Lord, give us hearts and minds that are humble enough to acknowledge our own limited understanding, and courageous enough to admit when we are wrong.

209

If you do something too good, then, after a while, if you don't watch it, you start showing off. And then you're not as good any more.

THE CATCHER IN THE RYE BY J. D. SALINGER, 1951

Pride goes before destruction,
    and a haughty spirit before a fall.

PROVERBS 16:18

Holy God, forgive us of the pride that blinds us to those around us and makes us strangers to our true identities.

210

Many years have passed since that night. The wall of the staircase up which I had watched the light of his candle gradually climb was long ago demolished. And in myself, too, many things have perished which I imagined would last for ever, and new ones have arisen, giving birth to new sorrows and new joys which in those days I could not have foreseen, just as now the old are hard to understand.

SWANN'S WAY BY MARCEL PROUST, 1913

My mouth will tell of your righteous acts,
   of your deeds of salvation all day long,
   though their number is past my knowledge.

PSALM 71:15

Holy God, our lives and your hand upon them stretch beyond our comprehension, but we lift up our gratitude for your abundant care on our past, our present, and our future.

211

Beauty means the scent of roses and then the death of roses.

THIS SIDE OF PARADISE BY F. SCOTT FITZGERALD, 1920

We do not live to ourselves, and we do not die to ourselves. If we live, we live to the Lord, and if we die, we die to the Lord; so then, whether we live or whether we die, we are the Lord's. For to this end Christ died and lived again, so that he might be Lord of both the dead and the living.

ROMANS 14:7–9

Lord, we know that death is a natural part of this life. Remind us that we belong to you in life and death, and help us to live as though we remember this.

212

In April I walked to the Adams' woods. The grass had greened one morning when I blinked; I missed it again. . . .

The morning woods were utterly new. A strong yellow light pooled between the trees; my shadow appeared and vanished on the path, since a third of the trees I walked under were still bare, a third spread a luminous haze wherever they grew, and another third blocked the sun with new, whole leaves.

PILGRIM AT TINKER CREEK BY ANNIE DILLARD, 1974

See, the former things have come to pass,
    and new things I now declare;
before they spring forth,
    I tell you of them.

ISAIAH 42:9

Lord God, there are times when change comes to us in ways we didn't foresee and couldn't have hoped for. We are so grateful for these surprises.

213

O thou bright jewel in my aim I strive
   To comprehend thee. Thine own words declare
Wisdom is higher than a fool can reach.
I cease to wonder, and no more attempt
Thine height t'explore, or fathom thy profound.
But, O my soul, sink not into despair,
Virtue is near thee, and with gentle hand
Would now embrace thee, hovers o'er thine head.

FROM "ON VIRTUE" BY PHILLIS WHEATLEY, 1773

The fear of the LORD is the beginning of wisdom,
   and the knowledge of the Holy One is insight.

PROVERBS 9:10

*Holy God, we humble ourselves before you, knowing that
we need not come to you with much wisdom and talent and
strength; instead we need come to you only with hearts ready to
hear your word.*

214

But when a soul, by choice and conscience, doth
Throw out her full force on another soul,
The conscience and the concentration both
Make mere life, Love. For Life in perfect whole
And aim consummated, is Love in sooth,
As nature's magnet-heat rounds pole with pole.

FROM "LOVE" BY ELIZABETH
BARRETT BROWNING, 1850

Little children, let us love, not in word or speech, but in truth and action.

1 JOHN 3:18

God of Love, fill us with a transforming love that bears itself out in both word and deed.

215

And then I happened to look around, and see that paper. It was a close place. I took it up, and held it in my hand. I was a trembling, because I'd got to decide, forever, betwixt two things, and I knowed it. I studied a minute, sort of holding my breath, and then says to myself: "All right, then, I'll go to hell"— and tore it up.

THE ADVENTURES OF HUCKLEBERRY FINN BY MARK TWAIN, 1884

But even if you do suffer for doing what is right, you are blessed. Do not fear what they fear, and do not be intimidated.

1 PETER 3:14

Lord, help me to do what is right, no matter how unpopular.
Show me the humanity in all people, that I may love as you love.

216

I am invisible, understand, simply because people refuse to see me. . . . When they approach me they see only my surroundings, themselves, or figments of their imagination—indeed, everything and anything except me.

INVISIBLE MAN BY RALPH ELLISON, 1952

We love because he first loved us. Those who say, "I love God," and hate their brothers or sisters, are liars; for those who do not love a brother or sister whom they have seen, cannot love God whom they have not seen.

1 JOHN 4:19–20

God, forgive us for not seeing each other, and may we not deceive ourselves into thinking that we can love you if we don't also love our neighbor.

217

O greater Maker of this Thy great sun,
  Give me the strength this one day's race to run,
Fill me with light, fill me with sun-like strength,
Fill me with joy to rob the day its length.
Light from within, light that will outward shine,
Strength to make strong some weaker heart than mine,
Joy to make glad each soul that feels its touch;
Great Father of the sun, I ask this much.

FROM "PRAYER AT SUNRISE" BY
JAMES WELDON JOHNSON, 1917

In the heavens he has set a tent for the sun,
  which comes out like a bridegroom from his
        wedding canopy,
    and like a strong man runs its course with joy.
Its rising is from the end of the heavens,
    and its circuit to the end of them;
    and nothing is hid from its heat.

PSALM 19:4B-6

Great Light of Lights, fill us with your radiance and help us to run our course with joy.

218

The old man opened the *North American* again, and read a few lines. "If we have ever had any virtue amongst us, we had better keep hold of it now," he said. He was not quoting.

THE EUROPEANS BY HENRY JAMES, 1878

I hereby command you: Be strong and courageous; do not be frightened or dismayed, for the LORD your God is with you wherever you go.

JOSHUA 1:9

Holy Lord, grant us strength to live our lives with courage and integrity, no matter the unknowns or evils we face.

219

It is the unknown we fear when we look upon death and darkness, nothing more.

HARRY POTTER AND THE HALF-BLOOD PRINCE BY J. K. ROWLING, 2005

The last enemy to be destroyed is death. For "God has put all things in subjection under his feet."

1 CORINTHIANS 15:26–27A

Lord of Life and Death, help us to understand that death and darkness no longer have power over us, for you have vanquished them for all time.

220

Freedom now appeared, to disappear no more forever. It was heard in every sound and seen in every thing. It was present to torment me with a sense of my wretched condition. I saw nothing without seeing it, I heard nothing without hearing it, and felt nothing without feeling it. It looked from every star, it smiled in every calm, breathed in every wind, and moved in every storm.

NARRATIVE OF THE LIFE OF FREDERICK DOUGLASS,
AN AMERICAN SLAVE BY FREDERICK DOUGLASS, 1845

Thus says the LORD:
    Maintain justice, and do what is right,
for soon my salvation will come,
    and my deliverance be revealed.

ISAIAH 56:1

Lord God, in the places where oppression seems to reign, we ask that your hand of justice would move to bring redemption and renewal.

-:⟶ ⁂ ⟵:-

As soon as the wood was silent again Susan and Lucy crept out into the open hill-top. The moon was getting low and thin clouds were passing across her, but still they could see the shape of the great Lion lying dead in his bonds. And down they both knelt in the wet grass and kissed his cold face and stroked his beautiful fur—what was left of it—and cried till they could cry no more. . . .

I hope no one who reads this book has been quite as miserable as Susan and Lucy were that night; but if you have been—if you've been up all night and cried till you have no more tears left in you—you will know that there comes in the end a sort of quietness. You feel as if nothing was ever going to happen again.

THE LION, THE WITCH, AND THE
WARDROBE BY C. S. LEWIS, 1950

I am poured out like water,
    and all my bones are out of joint;
my heart is like wax;
    it is melted within my breast.

PSALM 22:14

Christ, Man of Sorrows, meet all those whose hearts are heavy and despairing, and carry them in their suffering.

222

Have no fear of robbers or murderers. They are external dangers, petty dangers. We should fear ourselves. Prejudices are the real robbers; vices the real murderers. The great dangers are within us. Why worry about what threatens our heads or our purses? Let us think instead of what threatens our souls.

LES MISÉRABLES BY VICTOR HUGO, 1862

What then? Are we any better off? No, not at all; for we have already charged that all, both Jews and Greeks, are under the power of sin, as it is written:
"There is no one who is righteous not even one;
    there is no one who has understanding,
there is no one who seeks God."

ROMANS 3:9–11

Holy Father, we confess that we are sinners, so often filled with thoughts, words, or actions that are unkind and self-serving. Forgive us, and transform us through the power of Christ.

223

When they left the rock or tree or sand dune that had sheltered them for the night, the Navajo was careful to obliterate every trace of their temporary occupation. He buried the embers of the fire and the remnants of food, unpiled any stones he had piled together, filled up the holes he had scooped in the sand. . . . It was the Indian's way to pass through a country without disturbing anything; to pass and leave no trace, like fish through the water, or birds through the air.

DEATH COMES FOR THE ARCHBISHOP BY WILLA CATHER, 1927

The earth is the LORD's and all that is in it,
   the world, and those who live in it;
for he has founded it on the seas,
   and established it on the rivers.

PSALM 24:1-2

God of all, give us respect and care for your world, and may we walk humbly on the earth.

224

Good news and bad may bear the self-same knife;
  And death may follow both upon their flight;
For hearts that shrink or swell, alike will break.
Let then thy beauty, to preserve my life,
  Temper the source of this supreme delight,
  Lest joy so poignant slay a soul so weak.

FROM SONNET XXVI BY
MICHELANGELO BUONARROTI, 1623

Hear my prayer, O Lord,
  and give ear to my cry;
  do not hold your peace at my tears.
For I am your passing guest,
  an alien, like all my forebears.
Turn your gaze away from me, that I may smile again,
  before I depart and am no more.

PSALM 39:12–13

Lord, we are weak, and you are beyond our comprehension. May we forever walk humbly with you.

225

Our weakness should not terrify us: it is the source of our strength. . . . Power is made perfect in infirmity, and our very helplessness is all the more potent a claim on that Divine Mercy Who calls to Himself the poor, the little ones, the heavily burdened.

THE SEVEN STOREY MOUNTAIN BY THOMAS MERTON, 1948

But he said to me, "My grace is sufficient for you, for power is made perfect in weakness." So, I will boast all the more gladly of my weaknesses, so that the power of Christ may dwell in me.

2 CORINTHIANS 12:9

Lord Christ, you call those who are weary and heavy-laden to find their rest in you. Help us to look to your promises and not to our own weakness.

226

Some people's blameless lives are to blame for a good deal.

GAUDY NIGHT BY DOROTHY L. SAYERS, 1935

So, for the sake of your tradition, you make void the word of God. You hypocrites! Isaiah prophesied rightly about you when he said:
   "This people honors me with their lips,
      but their hearts are far from me;
   in vain do they worship me,
      teaching human precepts as doctrines."

MATTHEW 15:6–9

Lord Christ, guard us from religion which is far from you, and forgive us for mixing your kingdom with our own selfish aims.

227

The question, O me! so sad, recurring—What good amid
these, O me, O life?
Answer.
That you are here—that life exists, and identity;
That the powerful play goes on, and you will contribute
a verse.

FROM *LEAVES OF GRASS* BY WALT WHITMAN, 1855

Now the word of the LORD came to me saying,
"Before I formed you in the womb I knew you,
and before you were born I consecrated you;
I appointed you a prophet to the nations."

JEREMIAH 1:4–5

*Holy Father, we thank you that in you we find our meaning, our
naming, and our value.*

228

I t makes a difference, doesn't it, whether we fully fence ourselves in, or whether we are fenced out by the barriers of
others?

A ROOM WITH A VIEW BY E. M. FORSTER, 1908

I will deal with all your oppressors
    at that time.
And I will save the lame
    and gather the outcast,
and I will change their shame
    and renown in all the earth.
At that time I will bring you home,
    at the time when I gather you.

ZEPHANIAH 3:19–20A

*Holy Father, we praise you that however we may wall ourselves
off from the world, or however others do us harm, you are the
God of welcome, of healing, and of renewal.*

G od has made us so that we must be mutually dependent. We may ignore our own dependence, or refuse to acknowledge that others depend upon us in more respects than the payment of weekly wages; but the things must be, nevertheless. Neither you nor any other master can help yourselves. The most proudly independent man depends on those around him for their insensible influence on his character—his life.

NORTH AND SOUTH BY ELIZABETH GASKELL, 1854–55

Two are better than one, because they have a good reward for their toil. For if they fall, one will lift up the other; but woe to one who is alone and falls and does not have another to help.

ECCLESIASTES 4:9–10

Holy Father, forgive us for separating ourselves from community, for thinking it is a sign of weakness to need other people rather than recognizing that need as innate to our humanity.

230

It's by understanding me, and the boys, and mother, that you have helped me. I expect that is the only way one person ever really can help another.

O PIONEERS! BY WILLA CATHER, 1913

If then there is any encouragement in Christ, any consolation from love, any sharing in the Spirit, any compassion and sympathy, make my joy complete: be of the same mind, having the same love, being in full accord and of one mind.

PHILIPPIANS 2:1-2

Help us, O God, to live in love, to help each other, and to serve you all the rest of our days.

231

--•------ ✳ ------•--

The Psalmists in telling everyone to praise God are doing what all men do when they speak of what they care about. . . .

I think we delight to praise what we enjoy because the praise not merely expresses but completes the enjoyment; it is its appointed consummation. It is not out of compliment that lovers keep telling one another how beautiful they are; the delight is incomplete till it is expressed.

REFLECTIONS ON THE PSALMS BY C. S. LEWIS, 1958

O magnify the LORD with me,
   and let us exalt his name together.

. . . .

O taste and see that the LORD is good;
   happy are those who take refuge in him.

PSALM 34:3, 8

Holy God, we praise you for the world you have made, for the gift of life, and above all for your love and forgiveness, made known to us through Christ our Lord.

232

But secondly you say "society must exact vengeance, and society must punish." Wrong on both counts. Vengeance comes from the individual and punishment from God.

THE LAST DAY OF A CONDEMNED MAN BY VICTOR HUGO, 1829

I will seek the lost, and I will bring back the strayed, and I will bind up the injured, and I will strengthen the weak, but the fat and the strong I will destroy. I will feed them with justice.

EZEKIEL 34:16

Holy God, in the face of wrongs, of sins, of brokenness, may we trust that you are the God of justice and healing.

233

I would like to proclaim one of the things of which I am igno-rant, to publish a crucial indecision in my thinking, in order to see if some other doubter may help me to doubt, and the half-light we share turn into light.

"AN INVESTIGATION OF THE WORD"
BY JORGE LUIS BORGES, 1927

Bear one another's burdens, and in this way you will fulfill the law of Christ.

GALATIANS 6:2

Our Lord, may we be open and honest about our doubts, so that we may accompany each other and find our hearts encouraged.

Don't you see that all this leads to comfort in the end? It is part of the battle against sameness. Differences—eternal differences, planted by God in a single family, so that there may always be colour; sorrow perhaps, but colour in the daily grey.

HOWARD'S END BY E. M. FORSTER, 1910

For as in one body we have many members, and not all the members have the same function, so we, who are many, are one body in Christ, and individually we are members one of another.

ROMANS 12:4–5

O God, you fill the world with diverse talents, personalities, affections, and dreams. We praise you for this rich and varied world!

235

L ove takes off the masks that we fear we cannot live without
and know we cannot live within.

THE FIRE NEXT TIME BY JAMES BALDWIN, 1963

Beloved, let us love one another, because love is from God;
everyone who loves is born of God and knows God. . . . No
one has ever seen God; if we love one another, God lives in
us, and his love is perfected in us.

1 JOHN 4:7, 12

*Lord, thank you for your perfect love for us—all of us. Please
help us to love each other—and ourselves—as you love us.*

236

Who hath not learned, in hours of faith,
    The truth to flesh and sense unknown,
That Life is ever lord of Death,
    And Love can never lose its own!

FROM *SNOW-BOUND: A WINTER IDYLL* BY
JOHN GREENLEAF WHITTIER, 1866

I am the good shepherd. The good shepherd lays down his life for the sheep. . . .

    . . . My sheep hear my voice. I know them, and they follow me. I give them eternal life, and they will never perish. No one will snatch them out of my hand.

JOHN 10:11, 27–28

Lord Christ, we lift our hearts in gratitude for your faithful love that binds our hearts to you.

237

If you haven't already, you will lose someone you can't live without, and your heart will be badly broken, and you never completely get over the loss of a deeply beloved person. But this is also good news. The person lives forever, in your broken heart that doesn't seal back up. And you come through, and you learn to dance with the banged-up heart.

PLAN B: FURTHER THOUGHTS ON FAITH BY ANNE LAMOTT, 2005

When Mary came where Jesus was and saw him, she knelt at his feet and said to him, "Lord, if you had been here, my brother would not have died." When Jesus saw her weeping, and the Jews who came with her also weeping, he was greatly disturbed in spirit and deeply moved. He said, "Where have you laid him?" They said to him, "Lord, come and see." Jesus began to weep.

JOHN 11:32–35

Man of Sorrows, you knew grief and you wept over the body of your friend. Accompany us in our own grief and loss, we pray.

238

"How despicably I have acted!" she cried.—"I, who have prided myself on my discernment!—I, who have valued myself on my abilities! who have often disdained the generous candour of my sister, and gratified my vanity, in useless or blameable distrust.—How humiliating is this discovery!—Yet, how just a humiliation!—Had I been in love, I could not have been more wretchedly blind. But vanity, not love, has been my folly.—Pleased with the preference of one, and offended by the neglect of the other, on the very beginning of our acquaintance, I have courted prepossession and ignorance, and driven reason away, where either were concerned. Till this moment, I never knew myself."

PRIDE AND PREJUDICE BY JANE AUSTEN, 1813

The more words, the more vanity, so how is one the better? For who knows what is good for mortals while they live the few days of their vain life, which they pass like a shadow? For who can tell them what will be after them under the sun?

ECCLESIASTES 6:11–12

God of Wisdom and Truth, help us to uncover the lies we tell ourselves so that we may live in reality instead of vanity, and serve only you.

239

I say, beware of all enterprises that require new clothes, and not rather a new wearer of clothes. If there is not a new man, how can the new clothes be made to fit?

WALDEN BY HENRY DAVID THOREAU, 1854

That is not the way you learned Christ! For surely you have heard about him and were taught in him, as truth is in Jesus. You were taught to put away your former way of life, your old self, corrupt and deluded by its lusts, and to be renewed in the spirit of your minds, and to clothe yourselves with the new self, created according to the likeness of God in true righteousness and holiness.

EPHESIANS 4:20-24

Make me new, Lord, and clothe me in truth and righteousness, that I may do your will.

240

What is saving my life now is the conviction that there is no spiritual treasure to be found apart from the bodily experiences of human life on earth. My life depends on engaging the most ordinary physical activities with the most exquisite attention I can give them. My life depends on ignoring all touted distinctions between the secular and the sacred, the physical and the spiritual, the body and the soul. What is saving my life now is becoming more fully human, trusting that there is no way to God apart from real life in the real world.

AN ALTAR IN THE WORLD: A GEOGRAPHY OF FAITH BY BARBARA BROWN TAYLOR, 2009

I come to my garden, my sister, my bride;
    I gather my myrrh with my spice,
    I eat my honeycomb with my honey,
    I drink my wine with my milk.
Eat, friends, drink,
    and be drunk with love.

SONG OF SOLOMON 5:1

O God, you see that we live in the real world, in the senses, in the here and now. Help us to know the spiritual treasure sown in this real world, in the many beautiful things of this life, that we may know you fully and love you completely.

241

For what we suppose to be our love or our jealousy is never a single, continuous and indivisible passion. It is composed of an infinity of successive loves, of different jealousies, each of which is ephemeral, although by their uninterrupted multiplicity they give us the impression of continuity, the illusion of unity.

SWANN'S WAY BY MARCEL PROUST, 1913

Heaven and earth will pass away, but my words will not pass away.

MATTHEW 24:35

Lord of all, our lives are fleeting. In all that we are not, we look to what you are, eternal and unchanging.

242

Who alone suffers suffers most i' th' mind,
Leaving free things and happy shows behind;
But then the mind much sufferance doth o'erskip
When grief hath mates, and bearing fellowship.

KING LEAR BY WILLIAM SHAKESPEARE, 1606

Some friends play at friendship
but a true friend sticks closer than one's nearest kin.

PROVERBS 18:24

Holy Friend, thank you for companions earthly and divine who know us and love us and accompany us in joy and sadness.

243

You cannot conceive, nor can I, of the appalling strangeness of the mercy of God.

BRIGHTON ROCK BY GRAHAM GREENE, 1938

I am grateful to Christ Jesus our Lord, who has strengthened me, because he judged me faithful and appointed me to his service, even though I was formerly a blasphemer, a persecutor, and a man of violence. But I received mercy because I had acted ignorantly in unbelief, and the grace of our Lord overflowed for me with the faith and love that are in Christ Jesus.

1 TIMOTHY 1:12–14

Merciful God, thank you for loving us in our error and in our truth, and for drawing us ever closer to you.

244

All people of broad, strong sense have an instinctive repugnance to the men of maxims; because such people early discern that the mysterious complexity of our life is not to be embraced by maxims, and that to lace ourselves up in formulas of that sort is to repress all the divine promptings and inspirations that spring from growing insight and sympathy. And the man of maxims is the popular representative of the minds that are guided in their moral judgment solely by general rules, thinking that these will lead them to justice by a ready-made patent method, without the trouble of exerting patience, discrimination, impartiality.

THE MILL ON THE FLOSS BY GEORGE ELIOT, 1860

I still have many things to say to you, but you cannot bear them now. When the Spirit of truth comes, he will guide you into all the truth; for he will not speak on his own, but will speak whatever he hears, and he will declare to you the things that are to come.

JOHN 16:12–13

Holy Spirit, this world can be so confusing, the needs of each day so varied and complex. Let us look not for simple solutions but for your promised guidance and presence.

245

The pleasure of eating should be an *extensive* pleasure, not that of the mere gourmet. People who know the garden in which their vegetables have grown and know that the garden is healthy will remember the beauty of the growing plants, perhaps in the dewy first light of morning when gardens are at their best. Such a memory involves itself with the food and is one of the pleasures of eating.

"THE PLEASURES OF EATING" BY WENDELL BERRY, 1989

You cause grass to grow for the cattle,
    and plants for people to use,
to bring forth food from the earth,
    and wine to gladden the human heart,
oil to make the face shine,
    and bread to strengthen the human heart.

PSALM 104:14-15

O Lord, we are grateful for the abundant gifts of the world around us. Let us take notice of them.

246

Although claiming my true identity as a child of God, I still live as though the God to whom I am returning demands an explanation. I still think about his love as conditional and about home as a place I am not yet fully sure of. While walking home, I keep entertaining doubts about whether I will be truly welcome when I get there.

THE RETURN OF THE PRODIGAL SON BY HENRI NOUWEN, 1992

> There is no fear in love, but perfect love casts out fear; for fear has to do with punishment, and whoever fears has not reached perfection in love.
>
> 1 JOHN 4:18

Holy Father, it can be hard to believe that you can really accept us in all our sin and inconstancy. We acknowledge that you do not see things as we do, that you have called us Beloved simply because you love us, and not because of how lovable we are.

247

Compassion means to suffer with, but it doesn't mean to get lost in the suffering, so that it becomes exclusively one's own. I tend to do this, to replace the person for whom I am feeling compassion with myself. . . . It is not that in compassion one cuts oneself off from feeling, only from one's selfishness, self-centeredness.

CIRCLE OF QUIET BY MADELEINE L'ENGLE, 1972

Blessed be the God and Father of our Lord Jesus Christ, the Father of mercies and the God of all consolation, who consoles us in all our affliction, so that we may be able to console those who are in any affliction with the consolation with which we ourselves are consoled by God.

2 CORINTHIANS 1:3–4

Lord of Love, may our care for others not be cloaked self-interest, but instead may it truly and fundamentally be directed toward recognizing the needs of those around us.

What needs to be discharged is the intolerable tenderness of the past, the past gone and grieved over and never made sense of. Music ransoms us from the past, declares an amnesty, brackets and sets aside the old puzzles. Sing a new song.

LOVE IN THE RUINS BY WALKER PERCY, 1971

Do not remember the former things,
  or consider the things of old.

ISAIAH 43:18

Deliver us, Lord, from the mistakes and heartache of the past. Help us to sing a new song, to begin a new journey, to love and serve only you.

249

Adversity had not only ruined him, it had frightened him, and he was evidently going through his remnant of life on tiptoe, for fear of waking up the hostile fates.

THE AMBASSADORS BY HENRY JAMES, 1903

I have said this to you, so that in me you may have peace. In the world you face persecution. But take courage; I have conquered the world!

JOHN 16:33

Our Lord Christ, even though it is so easy to go through life anticipating hardships, we ask that you would embolden us. May we be not only healed but also strengthened, so we may live our lives in freedom from fear.

250

They caught up with each other's news casually, leaving long, cosy gaps of silence in which to go to work on their muffins and coffees. Jerome—after two months of having to be witty and brilliant in a strange town among strangers—appreciated the gift of it. People talk about the happy quiet that can exist between two lovers, but this too was great; sitting between his sister and his brother, saying nothing, eating.

ON BEAUTY BY ZADIE SMITH, 2005

How very good and pleasant it is
    when kindred live together in unity!

PSALM 133:1

Lord, what a gift and a shelter it is to be with people with whom we feel at home!

251

-:———※———:-

If you stumble about believability, what are you living for? Love is hard to believe, ask any lover. Life is hard to believe, ask any scientist. God is hard to believe, ask any believer. What is your problem with hard to believe?

LIFE OF PI BY YANN MARTEL, 2001

Then he said to Thomas, "Put your finger here and see my hands. Reach out your hand and put it in my side. Do not doubt but believe." Thomas answered him, "My Lord and my God!" Jesus said to him, "Have you believed because you have seen me? Blessed are those who have not seen and yet have come to believe."

JOHN 20:27-29

Let my doubts lead to discovery, Lord, that I may know you.

252

Yet Lord restore thine image, heare my call:
And though my hard heart scarce to thee can grone,
Remember that thou once didst write in stone.

FROM "THE SINNER" BY GEORGE HERBERT, 1633

Immediately the father of the child cried out, "I believe; help my unbelief!"

MARK 9:24

Lord God, you breathe life into the dead, healing into the broken. Renew me, that I may see you.

253

For what are we born if not to aid one another?

FOR WHOM THE BELL TOLLS BY
ERNEST HEMINGWAY, 1940

Create in me a clean heart, O God,
  and put a new and right spirit within me.
Do not cast me away from your presence,
  and do not take your holy spirit from me.
Restore to me the joy of your salvation,
  and sustain in me a willing spirit.

PSALM 51:10–12

You, O Lord, are a God of love and justice. Put in us, we pray, a new and right spirit, that we may give ourselves for each other, as Jesus Christ, your Son, gave himself for us.

254

Those born to wealth, and who have the means of gratifying every wish, know not what is the real happiness of life, just as those who have been tossed on the stormy waters of the ocean on a few frail planks can alone realize the blessings of fair weather.

THE COUNT OF MONTE CRISTO BY ALEXANDRE DUMAS, 1844–45

As my life was ebbing away,
    I remembered the LORD;
and my prayer came to you,
    into your holy temple.
Those who worship vain idols
    forsake their true loyalty.
But I with the voice of thanksgiving
    will sacrifice to you.

JONAH 2:7–9A

Our Lord, in the hardships of our lives, we turn our eyes to you and hope for your salvation.

255

To those who have large capability of loving and suffering, united with great power of firm endurance, there comes a time in their woe, when they are lifted out of the contemplation of their individual case into a searching inquiry into the nature of their calamity, and the remedy (if remedy there be) which may prevent its recurrence to others as well as to themselves.

MARY BARTON BY ELIZABETH GASKELL, 1848

Surely it was for my welfare
    that I had great bitterness;
but you have held back my life
    from the pit of destruction,
for you have cast all my sins
    behind your back.
. . . .
The living, the living, they thank you,
    as I do this day;
fathers make known to children
    your faithfulness.

ISAIAH 38:17, 19

Great God of Blessing, we thank you and celebrate your steadfast love and faithfulness.

O ur life is a faint tracing on the surface of mystery. The surface of mystery is not smooth, any more than the planet is smooth; not even a single hydrogen atom is smooth, let alone a pine. . . . Mystery itself is as fringed and intricate as the shape of the air in time.

PILGRIM AT TINKER CREEK BY ANNIE DILLARD, 1974

He reveals deep and hidden things;
    he knows what is in the darkness,
    and light dwells with him.

DANIEL 2:22

Light of Lights, God who sees, we praise you for revealing to us your story. You are so near to us, yet so beyond our comprehension.

257

It's lovely to live on a raft. We had the sky, up there, all speckled with stars, and we used to lay on our backs and look up at them, and discuss about whether they was made, or only just happened—Jim he allowed they was made, but I allowed they happened; I judged it would have took too long to make so many.

THE ADVENTURES OF HUCKLEBERRY
FINN BY MARK TWAIN, 1884

He determines the number of the stars;
    he gives to all of them their names.
Great is our Lord, and abundant in power;
    his understanding is beyond measure.

PSALM 147:4-5

Creator God who flung the stars, we give thanks for all the
beauty you have given us.

258

I would ask you to believe that he has a heart he very, very seldom reveals, and that there are deep wounds in it. My dear, I have seen it bleeding.

A TALE OF TWO CITIES BY CHARLES DICKENS, 1859

The heart knows its own bitterness,
and no stranger shares its joy.

PROVERBS 14:10

Loving Father, may we give our attention to the varied and mysterious lives of those we meet today, and may we honor their stories, see their heartaches and joys.

259

That's what art *is*, he said, the story of a life in all its particularity. It's the only thing that really is particular and personal. It's the expression and, at the same time, the fabric of the particular. . . .

. . . The secret story is the one we'll never know, although we're living it from day to day, thinking we're alive, thinking we've got it all under control and the stuff we overlook doesn't matter. But every single damn thing matters! Only we don't realize. We just tell ourselves that art runs on one track and life, our lives, on another, and we don't realize that's a lie.

LAST EVENINGS ON EARTH BY ROBERTO BOLAÑO, 1997

Above all, clothe yourselves with love, which binds everything together in perfect harmony.

COLOSSIANS 3:14

God of all stories, we delight in the multitude of stories that make up our lives. Help us to view each other's stories in love, and to receive them with compassion.

260

I can't help but wonder that maybe we need these kinds of moments. Not moments of quiet, but moments when our lives are upended by violent tragedy, monsters, zombies, because without them, how would we meet the men and women of our dreams, how would we make up for the sins of our pasts, how would we show our true natures—brave, caring, strong, intelligent?

I wonder, how would we?

"ESCAPE FROM THE MALL" BY MANUEL GONZALES, 2013

Then I saw a new heaven and a new earth; for the first heaven and the first earth had passed away, and the sea was no more. And I saw the holy city, the new Jerusalem, coming down out of heaven from God, prepared as a bride adorned for her husband. . . .

And the one who was seated on the throne said, "See, I am making all things new."

REVELATION 21:1-2, 5A

Help us, Lord, to see how we are being transformed in all the events of our lives, the joys and sorrows and horrors, for in you all things are transformed to beauty and light.

261

Don't you think there are two great things in life that we ought to aim at—truth and kindness? Let's have both if we can, but let's be sure of having one or the other.

THE LONGEST JOURNEY BY E. M. FORSTER, 1907

Do not let loyalty and faithfulness forsake you;
    bind them around your neck,
    write them on the tablet of your heart.
So you will find favor and good repute
    in the sight of God and of people.

PROVERBS 3:3–4

God, make us faithful to you, that we may live in truth and kindness.

262

The difference is that these young people take it for granted that they're going to get whatever they want, and that we almost always took it for granted that we shouldn't. Only, I wonder—the thing one's so certain of in advance: can it ever make one's heart beat as wildly?

THE AGE OF INNOCENCE BY EDITH WHARTON, 1920

Now faith is the assurance of things hoped for, the conviction of things not seen.

HEBREWS 11:1

Holy One, help us to have faith in your ultimate goodness. We know what we want, but we also know that our knowledge is incomplete. Grant us freedom from fear, for we know your love is everlasting.

263

I lifted my head, my boy, and looked around, and everything was so beautiful that it couldn't be put into words, so I just sighed. It was still and quiet, the air was light, and the grass was growing. . . . Grow, God's grass, grow! . . . A bird sang. . . . Sing, you little bird of God! . . . A little babe squeaked in a woman's arms. . . . God bless you, little man, grow and be happy, dear child! . . . And if there's mystery in the world, it only makes it even better; it fills the heart with awe and wonder, and it gladdens the heart.

THE ADOLESCENT BY FYODOR DOSTOEVSKY, 1875

You crown the year with your bounty;
   your wagon tracks overflow with richness.
The pastures of the wilderness overflow,
   the hills gird themselves with joy,
the meadows clothe themselves with flocks,
   the valleys deck themselves with grain,
   they shout and sing together for joy.

PSALM 65:11–13

Lord of all, may our voices join with those of the world around us, responding to you in joy and love.

As Beth had hoped, the "tide went out easily," and in the dark hour before the dawn, on the bosom where she had drawn her first breath, she quietly drew her last, with no farewell but one loving look, one little sigh. With tears and prayers and tender hands, mother and sisters made her ready for the long sleep that pain would never mar again, seeing with grateful eyes the beautiful serenity that soon replaced the pathetic patience that had wrung their hearts so long, and feeling, with reverent joy, that to their darling death was a benignant angel, not a phantom full of dread.

LITTLE WOMEN BY LOUISA MAY ALCOTT, 1869

Those who go out weeping,
    bearing the seed for sowing,
shall come home with shouts of joy,
    carrying their sheaves.

PSALM 126:6

Lord Christ, defeater of death, carry us through our places of deep sorrow. May your promises be our hope, your love our comfort.

265

There is always something left to love.

ONE HUNDRED YEARS OF SOLITUDE
BY GABRIEL GARCÍA MÁRQUEZ, 1967

Thus says the LORD:
The people who survived the sword
found grace in the wilderness;
when Israel sought for rest,
the LORD appeared to him from far away.
I have loved you with an everlasting love;
therefore I have continued my faithfulness to you.

JEREMIAH 31:2–3

Our Lord and our God, we are grateful for your undeserved and unfailing love!

266

When I heard the learn'd astronomer,
    When the proofs, the figures, were ranged in columns
  before me,
When I was shown the charts and diagrams, to add, divide,
  and measure them,
When I sitting heard the astronomer where he lectured
  with much applause in the lecture-room,
How soon unaccountable I became tired and sick,
Till rising and gliding out I wander'd off by myself,
In the mystical moist night-air, and from time to time,
Look'd up in perfect silence at the stars.

"WHEN I HEARD THE LEARN'D ASTRONOMER"
BY WALT WHITMAN, 1867

Praise him, sun and moon;
    praise him, all you shining stars!
. . . .
Let them praise the name of the LORD,
    for he commanded and they were created.

PSALM 148:3, 5

Maker of all things, may we listen to the voice of creation praising you. May we join it.

267

See, you don't have to think about doing the right thing. If you're for the right thing, then you do it without thinking.

I KNOW WHY THE CAGED BIRD SINGS BY MAYA ANGELOU, 1969

For you were called to freedom, brothers and sisters; only do not use your freedom as an opportunity for self-indulgence, but through love become slaves to one another. For the whole law is summed up in a single commandment, "You shall love your neighbor as yourself." If, however, you bite and devour one another, take care that you are not consumed by one another.

GALATIANS 5:13–15

Holy One, help us to know the right thing and do the right thing, loving our neighbors as ourselves, and you, totally and completely.

268

"Stay!" said Mr. Hale, hurrying to the book-shelves. "Mr. Higgins! I'm sure you'll join us in family prayer?" . . .

Margaret the Churchwoman, her father the Dissenter, Higgins the Infidel, knelt down together. It did them no harm.

NORTH AND SOUTH BY ELIZABETH GASKELL, 1854–55

Now I appeal to you, brothers and sisters, by the name of our Lord Jesus Christ, that all of you be in agreement and that there be no divisions among you, but that you be united in the same mind and the same purpose.

1 CORINTHIANS 1:10

Our Lord, let us be brave and gracious in relationships with people who are not like us. Help us to see each other.

269

During the confusion and bewilderment of the second day Mary hid herself in the nursery and was forgotten by everyone. Nobody thought of her, nobody wanted her, and strange things happened of which she knew nothing. Mary alternately cried and slept through the hours. She only knew that people were ill and that she heard mysterious and frightening sounds. Once she crept into the dining-room and found it empty, though a partially finished meal was on the table and chairs and plates looked as if they had been hastily pushed back when the diners rose suddenly for some reason.

THE SECRET GARDEN BY FRANCES HODGSON BURNETT, 1911

How long, O LORD? Will you forget me forever?
How long will you hide your face from me?

PSALM 13:1

Lord, there are times I feel so alone. Help me to feel you at my side, to know your calming presence amid whatever trials I face.

270

The thing about light is that it really isn't yours; it's what you gather and shine back. And it gets more power from reflectiveness; if you sit still and take it in, it fills your cup, and then you can give it off yourself.

*TRAVELING MERCIES: SOME THOUGHTS
ON FAITH* BY ANNE LAMOTT, 1999

You are the light of the world. A city built on a hill cannot be hid. No one after lighting a lamp puts it under the bushel basket, but on the lampstand, and it gives light to all in the house. In the same way, let your light shine before others, so that they may see your good works and give glory to your Father in heaven.

MATTHEW 5:14–16

Light in the Darkness, illuminate us so that we may reflect your glory.

271

Where are the songs of Spring? Ay, where are they?
  Think not of them, thou hast thy music too—
While barred clouds bloom the soft-dying day,
And touch the stubble-plains with rosy hue.

FROM "TO AUTUMN" BY JOHN KEATS, 1820

Like the cold of snow in the time of harvest
  are faithful messengers to those who send them;
  they refresh the spirit of their masters.

PROVERBS 25:13

Lord God, may our words be meaningful, bringing refreshment to those who hear them.

272

We could never have loved the earth so well if we had had no childhood in it, if it were not the earth where the same flowers come up again every spring that we used to gather with our tiny fingers as we sat lisping to ourselves on the grass, the same hips and haws on the autumn hedgerows, the same redbreasts that we used to call "God's birds" because they did no harm to the precious crops. What novelty is worth that sweet monotony where everything is known and loved because it is known?

THE MILL ON THE FLOSS BY GEORGE ELIOT, 1860

Look at the birds of the air; they neither sow nor reap nor gather into barns, and yet your heavenly Father feeds them. Are you not of more value than they?

MATTHEW 6:26

O Christ, in you we are fully known and fully loved, valued as members in your glorious creation.

273

It is not the tree that forsakes the flower, but the flower that forsakes the tree.

THE COUNT OF MONTE CRISTO BY
ALEXANDRE DUMAS, 1844–45

Abide in me as I abide in you. Just as the branch cannot bear fruit by itself unless it abides in the vine, neither can you unless you abide in me. I am the vine, you are the branches. Those who abide in me and I in them bear much fruit, because apart from me you can do nothing.

JOHN 15:4–5

Christ, we look to you as our Source, desiring to root the entirety of our lives in you.

274

-⁘----※----⁘-

There is no steady unretracing progress in this life; we do not advance through fixed gradations, and at the last one pause:—through infancy's unconscious spell, boyhood's thoughtless faith, adolescence' doubt (the common doom), then scepticism, then disbelief, resting at last in manhood's pondering repose of If. But once gone through, we trace the round again; and are infants, boys, and men, and Ifs eternally. Where lies the final harbor, whence we unmoor no more?

MOBY-DICK BY HERMAN MELVILLE, 1851

Not that I have already obtained this or have already reached the goal; but I press on to make it my own, because Christ Jesus has made me his own. Beloved, I do not consider that I have made it my own; but this one thing I do: forgetting what lies behind and straining forward to what lies ahead, I press on toward the goal for the prize of the heavenly call of God in Christ Jesus.

PHILIPPIANS 3:12–14

Lord Christ, give us patience and tenacity and trust as we journey toward fullness of life with you.

275

I suppose one reason why we are seldom able to comfort our neighbors with our words is that our goodwill gets adulterated, in spite of ourselves, before it can pass our lips. We can send black puddings and pettitoes without giving them a flavour of our own egoism; but language is a stream that is almost sure to smack of a mingled soil.

SILAS MARNER BY GEORGE ELIOT, 1861

You must understand this, my beloved: let everyone be quick to listen, slow to speak, slow to anger; for your anger does not produce God's righteousness.

JAMES 1:19–20

God who knows us all, give us pause in speaking too quickly with one another, and may we know that sometimes our listening will be the best comfort.

276

Thy life's a miracle. Speak yet again.

KING LEAR BY
WILLIAM SHAKESPEARE, 1606

O Lord, you have searched me and known me.
You know when I sit down and when I rise up;
   you discern my thoughts from far away.
You search out my path and my lying down,
   and are acquainted with all my ways.
Even before a word is on my tongue,
   O Lord, you know it completely.

PSALM 139:1–4

*We are astounded, Lord, that you know us and love us and
offer us this miraculous life. Thank you.*

277

When you encounter another person, when you have dealings with anyone at all, it is as if a question is being put to you. So you must think, What is the Lord asking of me in this moment, in this situation? If you confront insult or antagonism, your first impulse will be to respond in kind. But if you think, as it were, This is an emissary sent from the Lord, and some benefit is intended for me, first of all the occasion to demonstrate my faithfulness, the chance to show that I do in some small degree participate in the grace that saved me, you are free to act otherwise than as circumstances would seem to dictate. You are free to act by your own lights. You are freed at the same time of the impulse to hate or resent that person.

GILEAD BY MARILYNNE ROBINSON, 2004

Then Peter came and said to him, "Lord, if another member of the church sins against me, how often should I forgive? As many as seven times?" Jesus said to him, "Not seven times, but, I tell you, seventy-seven times."

MATTHEW 18:21–22

God, help us to forgive, as we expect to be forgiven. Give us strength to live together and love each other.

278

I wondered if that was how forgiveness budded; not with the fanfare of epiphany, but with pain gathering its things, packing up, and slipping away unannounced in the middle of the night.

THE KITE RUNNER BY KHALED HOSSEINI, 2003

But love your enemies, do good, and lend, expecting nothing in return. Your reward will be great, and you will be children of the Most High; for he is kind to the ungrateful and the wicked. Be merciful, just as your Father is merciful.

LUKE 6:35–36

You call us to live in community, Lord; help us to love and to set aside our hurt.

279

Every little trifle, for some reason, does seem incalculably important today, and when you say of a thing that "nothing hangs on it," it sounds like blasphemy. There's never any knowing—(how am I to put it?)—which of our actions, which of our idlenesses won't have things hanging on it for ever.

WHERE ANGELS FEAR TO TREAD BY E. M. FORSTER, 1905

Conduct yourselves wisely toward outsiders, making the most of the time. Let your speech always be gracious, seasoned with salt, so that you may know how you ought to answer everyone.

COLOSSIANS 4:5–6

Lord, help us to act wisely and with compassion, so that we may reflect your love and grace.

280

After a while, though the grief did not go away from us, it grew quiet. What had seemed a storm wailing through the entire darkness seemed to come in at last and lie down.

JAYBER CROW BY WENDELL BERRY, 2000

Then they cried to the LORD in their trouble,
  and he brought them out from their distress;
he made the storm be still,
  and the waves of the sea were hushed.

PSALM 107:28-29

Christ, our Brother and Companion on the way, bring us out of our distress and let us know the peace that only you can give.

281

The rising of the sun had made everything look so differ-ent—all the colours and shadows were changed—that for a moment they didn't see the important thing. Then they did. The Stone Table was broken into two pieces by a great crack that ran down it from end to end; and there was no Aslan. . . .

"Who's done it?" cried Susan. "What does it mean? Is it more magic?"

"Yes!" said a great voice behind their backs. "It is more magic." They looked round. There, shining in the sunrise, larger than they had seen him before, shaking his mane (for it had apparently grown again) stood Aslan himself.

"Oh Aslan!" cried both the children, staring up at him, almost as much frightened as they were glad.

"Aren't you dead then, dear Aslan?" said Lucy.

"Not now," said Aslan.

*THE LION, THE WITCH, AND THE
WARDROBE* BY C. S. LEWIS, 1950

The LORD, your God, is in your midst,
a warrior who gives victory.

ZEPHANIAH 3:17A

Lord Christ, we praise you for your victorious life that defeated sin and death!

282

That was a memorable day for me, for it made great changes in me. But it is the same with any life. Imagine one selected day struck out of it, and think how different its course would have been. Pause you who read this, and think for a moment of the long chain of iron or gold, of thorns or flowers, that would never have bound you, but for the formation of the first link on one memorable day.

GREAT EXPECTATIONS BY CHARLES DICKENS, 1860–61

But take care and watch yourselves closely, so as neither to forget the things that your eyes have seen nor to let them slip from your mind all the days of your life; make them known to your children and your children's children.

DEUTERONOMY 4:9

Holy Father, let us walk through our days with faith in your guidance in our humble lives, and with reverence for your constant presence with us.

283

So this is what I will do. I will gather together my past and look. I will see a thing that has already happened. The pain that cut my spirit loose. I will hold that pain in my hand until it becomes hard and shiny, more clear. And then my fierceness can come back, my golden side, my black side.

THE JOY LUCK CLUB BY AMY TAN, 1989

What then are we to say about these things? If God is for us, who is against us? . . . Who will separate us from the love of Christ? Will hardship, or distress, or persecution, or famine, or nakedness, or peril, or sword? . . . No, in all these things we are more than conquerors through him who loved us.

ROMANS 8:31, 35, 37

God, in you our pain is conquered and our distress set aside. Thank you that nothing can separate us from your love.

284

Anna spoke not only naturally and intelligently, but intelligently and casually, without attaching any value to her own thoughts, yet giving great value to the thoughts of the one she was talking to.

ANNA KARENINA BY LEO TOLSTOY, 1877

When words are many, transgression is not lacking,
   but the prudent are restrained in speech.

PROVERBS 10:19

Lord our God, teach us to listen quickly, rather than to insist that first our own words be heard. May our attentiveness honor the lives of those around us.

285

In the mansion called literature I would have the eaves deep and the walls dark, I would push back into the shadow the things that come forward too clearly, I would strip away the useless decoration. I do not ask that this be done everywhere, but perhaps we may be allowed at least one mansion where we can turn off the electric lights and see what it is like without them.

IN PRAISE OF SHADOWS BY JUN'ICHIRŌ TANIZAKI, 1933-34

The eye is the lamp of the body. So, if your eye is healthy, your whole body will be full of light.

MATTHEW 6:22

Lord of Light, give us eyes to see as you see, to pay attention and to be filled with wonder.

286

What I have said respecting and against religion, I mean strictly to apply to the slaveholding religion of this land, and with no possible reference to Christianity proper; for, between the Christianity of this land, and the Christianity of Christ, I recognize the widest possible difference—so wide, that to receive the one as good, pure, and holy, is of necessity to reject the other as bad, corrupt, and wicked. To be the friend of one, is of necessity to be the enemy of the other.

NARRATIVE OF THE LIFE OF FREDERICK DOUGLASS, AN AMERICAN SLAVE BY FREDERICK DOUGLASS, 1845

There is no longer Jew or Greek, there is no longer slave or free, there is no longer male and female; for all of you are one in Christ Jesus.

GALATIANS 3:28

Holy Lord, you are not the God of slavery but of freedom, and we look to you to bring your salvation into this world.

287

Jesu, thine all-victorious love
  Shed in my heart abroad!
Then shall my feet no longer rove,
Rooted and fixed in God.
. . . .
My steadfast soul, from falling free,
Shall then no longer move;
But Christ be all the world to me,
And all my heart be love.

"MY GOD! I KNOW, I FEEL THEE
MINE" BY CHARLES WESLEY, 1740

For you were going astray like sheep, but now you have
returned to the shepherd and guardian of your souls.

1 PETER 2:25

*Our Lord, we thank you that you are our Good Shepherd when
we lose our way, and even when we lose the will to seek after it.*

I n this world there are so many of these common coarse people, who have no picturesque sentimental wretchedness! It is so needful we should remember their existence, else we may happen to leave them quite out of our religion and philosophy and frame lofty theories which only fit a world of extremes.

ADAM BEDE BY GEORGE ELIOT, 1859

[Jesus] said also to the one who had invited him, "When you give a luncheon or a dinner, do not invite your friends or your brothers or your relatives or rich neighbors, in case they may invite you in return, and you would be repaid. But when you give a banquet, invite the poor, the crippled, the lame, and the blind. And you will be blessed, because they cannot repay you, for you will be repaid at the resurrection of the righteous."

LUKE 14:12-14

God who honors the lowly, teach us your economy, where the last are first, and the poor are rich. Free us from valuing others based on status, wealth, and influence. May we see others not for what they can do for us, but for their belovedness.

289

The beauty and mystery of this world only emerges through affection, attention, interest and compassion . . . open your eyes wide and actually see this world by attending to its colors, details and irony.

MY NAME IS RED BY ORHAN PAMUK, 1998

God thunders wondrously with his voice;
    he does great things that we cannot comprehend.
For to the snow he says, "Fall on the earth";
    and the shower of rain, his heavy shower of rain,
serves as a sign on everyone's hand,
    so that all whom he has made may know it.

JOB 37:5-7

Help us, Creator God, to see the many miracles and mysteries you have placed right in front of us, if we only have courage to see.

290

We work in the dark—we do what we can—we give what we have. Our doubt is our passion, and our passion is our task. The rest is the madness of art.

"THE MIDDLE YEARS" BY HENRY JAMES, 1893

For now we see in a mirror, dimly, but then we will see face to face. Now I know only in part; then I will know fully, even as I have been fully known.

1 CORINTHIANS 13:12

Lord God, you know us in the places where we don't even know ourselves. We praise you that you are not afraid of our doubt.

291

Self-rejection is the greatest enemy of the spiritual life because it contradicts the sacred voice that calls us the "Beloved." Being the Beloved expresses the core truth of our existence.

LIFE OF THE BELOVED BY HENRI NOUWEN, 1992

As indeed he says in Hosea,
"Those who were not my people I will call 'my people,'
    and her who was not beloved I will call 'beloved.'"
"And in the very place where it was said to them,
    'You are not my people,'
    there they shall be called children of the living God."

ROMANS 9:25-26

Our Lord Christ, we are filled with joy and gratitude at the ways in which you call us your own when we feel far from you, and call us beloved when we feel unlovable.

292

"They are afraid, Tayo. They feel something happening, they can see something happening around them, and it scares them. Indians or Mexicans or whites—most people are afraid of change. They think that if their children have the same color of skin, the same color of eyes, that nothing is changing." She laughed softly. "They are fools. They blame us, the ones who look different. That way they don't have to think about what has happened inside themselves."

CEREMONY BY LESLIE MARMON SILKO, 1977

Do not worry about anything, but in everything by prayer and supplication with thanksgiving let your requests be made known to God. And the peace of God, which surpasses all understanding, will guard your hearts and your minds in Christ Jesus.

PHILIPPIANS 4:6-7

Unchanging God, we know that the nature of life is change. Keep us secure in what does not change: your love and care for us.

293

It is impossible that there should be no servants in the world; but act so that your servant may be freer in spirit than if he were not a servant. And why cannot I be a servant to my servant and even let him see it, and that without any pride on my part or any mistrust on his?

THE BROTHERS KARAMAZOV BY FYODOR DOSTOEVSKY, 1880

The greatest among you must become like the youngest, and the leader like one who serves. For who is greater, the one who is at the table or the one who serves? Is it not the one at the table? But I am among you as one who serves.

LUKE 22:26B–27

Our Lord Christ, if you came as Servant of all, how much more should we humble ourselves to honor and serve those around us, regardless of their status or position? Help us when we resist following in your footsteps of self-giving.

294

A rt is for me the great integrator, and I understand Christianity as I understand art. I understand Christmas as I understand Bach's *Sleepers Awake* or *Jesu, Joy of Man's Desiring*; as I understand Braque's clowns, Blake's poetry. And I understand it when I am able to pray with the mind in the heart, as Theophan the Recluse advised. When we pray with the mind in the heart, sunside and nightside are integrated, we begin to heal, and we come close to the kind of understanding which can accept an unacceptable Christianity. When I am able to pray with the mind in the heart, I am joyfully able to affirm the irrationality of Christmas.

THE IRRATIONAL SEASON BY MADELEINE L'ENGLE, 1977

The people who walked in darkness
    have seen a great light;
those who lived in a land of deep darkness—
    on them light has shined.
. . . .
For a child has been born for us,
    a son given to us;
authority rests upon his shoulders;
    and he is named
Wonderful Counselor, Mighty God,
    Everlasting Father, Prince of Peace.

ISAIAH 9:2, 6

God with Us, we receive you, the Light of the World, into the humble darkness of our lives.

295

You think the dead we loved truly ever leave us? You think that we don't recall them more clearly in times of great trouble?

HARRY POTTER AND THE PRISONER OF
AZKABAN BY J. K. ROWLING, 1999

But we do not want you to be uninformed, brothers and sisters, about those who have died, so that you may not grieve as others do who have no hope. For since we believe that Jesus died and rose again, even so, through Jesus, God will bring with him those who have died

1 THESSALONIANS 4:13–14

God of the living and the dead, remind us that we are surrounded by a great cloud of witnesses, and that in times of trouble you—and they—are present to us.

296

People think pleasing God is all God cares about. But any fool living in the world can see it always trying to please us back.

THE COLOR PURPLE BY ALICE WALKER, 1982

You visit the earth and water it,
    you greatly enrich it;
the river of God is full of water;
. . . .
the meadows clothe themselves with flocks,
    the valleys deck themselves with grain,
    they shout and sing together for joy.

PSALM 65:9A, 13

Thank you, God, for the abundance of the world that reveals your delight in giving us good gifts.

297

No, no, 'tis all men's office to speak patience
To those that wring under the load of sorrow,
But no man's virtue nor sufficiency
To be so moral when he shall endure
The like himself. Therefore give me no counsel.
My griefs cry louder than advertisement.

MUCH ADO ABOUT NOTHING
BY WILLIAM SHAKESPEARE, 1612

Who is this that darkens counsel by words without knowledge?

JOB 38:2

Lord, in perilous times, help us to offer comfort and peace, and words that heal rather than harm.

298

I have discovered that most people have no one to talk to, no one, that is, who really wants to listen. When it does at last dawn on a man that you really want to hear about his business, the look that comes over his face is something to see.

THE MOVIEGOER BY WALKER PERCY, 1961

Search me, O God, and know my heart;
  test me and know my thoughts.
See if there is any wicked way in me,
  and lead me in the way everlasting.

PSALM 139:23-24

Help us, O God, to listen to others so that they know they are known and heard and loved, as you know and hear and love us.

299

The growing good of the world is partly dependent on unhistoric acts; and that things are not so ill with you and me as they might have been, is half owing to the number who lived faithfully a hidden life, and rest in unvisited tombs.

MIDDLEMARCH BY GEORGE ELIOT, 1871–72

The fruit of the Spirit is love, joy, peace, patience, kindness, generosity, faithfulness, gentleness, and self-control. There is no law against such things.

GALATIANS 5:22–23

Lord, thank you for those whose ordinary, hidden, and unrecognized virtues have blessed our lives in ways we can't even begin to know, and may our own lives bless others regardless of recognition.

300

Therefore my soul lay out of sight,
   Untun'd, unstrung:
My feeble spirit, unable to look right,
Like a nipt blossome, hung
Discontented.

O cheer and tune my heartless breast,
Deferre no time;
That so thy favours granting my request,
They and my minde may chime,
And mend my ryme.

FROM "DENIAL" BY
GEORGE HERBERT, 1633

Let me hear joy and gladness;
   let the bones that you have crushed rejoice.
. . . .
Create in me a clean heart, O God,
   and put a new and right spirit within me.

PSALM 51:8, 10

O Lord, we don't even have the words or strength to reach out to you. Meet us, meet us.

301

To matter in the scheme of the cosmos: this is better theology than all our sociology. It is, in fact, all that God has promised to us: that we matter. That he cares. As far as I know, no great prophet has promised people that God will give them social justice, though he may have threatened doom and extinction if the people themselves don't do something about it. If God cares about us, we have to care about each other.

Sociology is rational. God is not.

God knows the very moment we are born.

CIRCLE OF QUIET BY MADELEINE L'ENGLE, 1972

My frame was not hidden from you,
when I was being made in secret,
   intricately woven in the depths of the earth.
Your eyes beheld my unformed substance.
In your book were written
   all the days that were formed for me,
   when none of them as yet existed.

PSALM 139:15-16

Lord of all, we praise you for the bewildering and humbling reality that each of us, personally and distinctly, matter to you.

302

Yet even in the loneliness of the canyon I knew there were others like me who had brothers they did not understand but wanted to help. We are probably those referred to as "our brothers' keepers," possessed of one of the oldest and possibly one of the most futile and certainly one of the most haunting of instincts. It will not let us go.

A RIVER RUNS THROUGH IT AND OTHER STORIES BY NORMAN MACLEAN, 1976

Cain said to his brother Abel, "Let us go out to the field." And when they were in the field, Cain rose up against his brother Abel, and killed him. Then the LORD said to Cain, "Where is your brother Abel?" He said, "I do not know; am I my brother's keeper?" And the LORD said, "What have you done? Listen; your brother's blood is crying out to me from the ground!"

GENESIS 4:8–10

Lord, we know that we are our brothers' and sisters' keepers. Help us to have hearts of service so that we may help.

303

❧—※—❧

Most people guard and keep; they suppose that it is they themselves and what they identify with themselves that they are guarding and keeping, whereas what they are actually guarding and keeping is their system of reality and what they assume themselves to be. One can give nothing whatever without giving oneself—that is to say, risking oneself. If one cannot risk oneself, then one is simply incapable of giving. And, after all, one can give freedom only by setting someone free.

THE FIRE NEXT TIME BY JAMES BALDWIN, 1963

For through the law I died to the law, so that I might live to God. I have been crucified with Christ; and it is no longer I who live, but it is Christ who lives in me. And the life I now live in the flesh I live by faith in the Son of God, who loved me and gave himself for me.

GALATIANS 2:19-20

Loving Christ, you risked all that we might have eternal life. Grant me the courage to risk myself for the sake of others.

304

Love, sooner or later, forces us out of time. It does not accept that limit. Of all that we feel and do, all the virtues and all the sins, love alone crowds us at last over the edge of the world. For love is always more than a little strange here. It is not explainable or even justifiable. It is itself the justifier. We do not make it. If it did not happen to us, we could not imagine it. It includes the world and time as a pregnant woman includes her child whose wrongs she will suffer and forgive. It is in the world but is not altogether of it. It is of eternity. It takes us there when it most holds us here.

JAYBER CROW BY WENDELL BERRY, 2000

And now faith, hope, and love abide, these three; and the greatest of these is love.

1 CORINTHIANS 13:13

God of Love, fill us with compassion for the world you have created and the people who populate it, so that we may show the nations who you are.

305

I experience religious dread whenever I find myself thinking that I know the limits of God's grace, since I am utterly certain it exceeds any imagination a human being might have of it. God does, after all, so love the world.

"WONDROUS LOVE" BY MARILYNNE ROBINSON, 2012

For God so loved the world that he gave his only Son, so that everyone who believes in him may not perish but may have eternal life.

Indeed, God did not send the Son into the world to condemn the world, but in order that the world might be saved through him.

JOHN 3:16–17

Holy One, we give thanks for your grace and love, and for your Son, our Savior Jesus Christ.

306

When Levin thought what he was and what he was living for, he could find no answer to the questions and was reduced to despair; but when he left off questioning himself about it, it seemed as though he knew both what he was and what he was living for, acting and living resolutely and without hesitation.

ANNA KARENINA BY LEO TOLSTOY, 1877

Then I saw all the work of God, that no one can find out what is happening under the sun. However much they may toil in seeking, they will not find it out; even though those who are wise claim to know, they cannot find it out.

ECCLESIASTES 8:17

O God, in the midst of our confusion, and when life feels disappointing or void of meaning, we look to your love to be an anchor, even when we don't feel it.

307

L ife is so damned hard. . . . It just hurts people and hurts people, until finally it hurts them so that they can't be hurt ever any more. That's the last and worst thing it does.

THE BEAUTIFUL AND DAMNED BY F. SCOTT FITZGERALD, 1922

O taste and see that the LORD is good;
  happy are those who take refuge in him.
O fear the LORD, you his holy ones,
  for those who fear him have no want.
The young lions suffer want and hunger,
  but those who seek the LORD lack no good thing.

Come, O children, listen to me;
  I will teach you the fear of the LORD.

PSALM 34:8–11

In the face of suffering, O God of the brokenhearted, we put our trust in you. Rescue us, accompany us, and let us know your steadfast love.

308

Insight doesn't happen often on the click of the moment, like a lucky snapshot, but comes in its own time and more slowly and from nowhere but within. The sharpest recognition is surely that which is charged with sympathy as well as with shock—it is a form of human vision. And that is of course a gift.

THE EYE OF THE STORY: SELECTED ESSAYS AND REVIEWS BY EUDORA WELTY, 1978

With patience a ruler may be persuaded,
and a soft tongue can break bones.

PROVERBS 25:15

Holy One, give us vision, so that we may see the world as it is, and compassion, that we may love it as it is.

309

For one brief golden moment rare like wine,
  The gracious city swept across the line;
Oblivious of the color of my skin,
Forgetting that I was an alien guest,
She bent to me, my hostile heart to win,
Caught me in passion to her pillowy breast;
The great, proud city, seized with a strange love,
Bowed down for one flame hour my pride to prove.

"THE CITY'S LOVE" BY CLAUDE MCKAY, 1922

So he came and proclaimed peace to you who were far off
and peace to those who were near; for through him both
of us have access in one Spirit to the Father.

EPHESIANS 2:17–18

*God, help us to be peace to those near and far off, to offer love
to those of every color, and to render justice to the alien, as you
have taught us.*

It is the infirmity of our nature always to believe ourselves much more unhappy than those who groan by our sides.

THE COUNT OF MONTE CRISTO BY ALEXANDRE DUMAS, 1844–45

Now when Job's three friends heard of all these troubles that had come upon him, each of them set out from his home—Eliphaz the Temanite, Bildad the Shuhite, and Zophar the Naamathite. They met together to go and console and comfort him. When they saw him from a distance, they did not recognize him, and they raised their voices and wept aloud; they tore their robes and threw dust in the air upon their heads. They sat with him on the ground seven days and seven nights, and no one spoke a word to him, for they saw that his suffering was very great.

JOB 2:11–13

Lord, it is so easy to get tangled in thoughts about ourselves. Forgive us for the ways in which this blinds us to the people around us, and give us new sight to look outward in love.

311

❖───✳───❖

We do not content ourselves with the life we have in ourselves and in our own being; we desire to live an imaginary life in the mind of others, and for this purpose we endeavor to shine. We labor unceasingly to adorn and preserve this imaginary existence, and neglect the real.

PENSÉES BY BLAISE PASCAL, 1670

And whenever you pray, do not be like the hypocrites; for they love to stand and pray in the synagogues and at the street corners, so that they may be seen by others. Truly I tell you, they have received their reward. But whenever you pray, go into your room and shut the door and pray to your Father who is in secret; and your Father who sees in secret will reward you.

MATTHEW 6:5-6

Humble Christ, forgive us for living so much of existence in imaginary scenarios and perceptions. Teach us to be present, humble, and at peace as we make our home in you.

312

When she went out into the dark kitchen to fix her plants for the night, she used to stand by the window and look out at the white fields, or watch the currents of snow whirling over the orchard. She seemed to feel the weight of all the snow that lay down there. . . . And yet, down under the frozen crusts, at the roots of the trees, the secret of life was still safe, warm as the blood in one's heart; and the spring would come again! Oh, it would come again!

O PIONEERS! BY WILLA CATHER, 1913

The LORD will guide you continually,
    and satisfy your needs in parched places,
        and make your bones strong;
and you shall be like a watered garden,
    like a spring of water,
        whose waters never fail.

ISAIAH 58:11

Praise be to you, O God. From the winter's cold, you bring new life, and from the deserts, you bring springs of water.

313

What do we find God "doing about" this business of sin and evil? . . . God did not abolish the fact of evil; He transformed it. He did not stop the Crucifixion; He rose from the dead.

"THE TRIUMPH OF EASTER" BY DOROTHY L. SAYERS, 1938

For the one who sanctifies and those who are sanctified all have one Father. For this reason Jesus is not ashamed to call them brothers and sisters. . . .

Since, therefore, the children share flesh and blood, he himself likewise shared the same things, so that through death he might destroy the one who has the power of death, that is, the devil, and free those who all their lives were held in slavery by the fear of death.

HEBREWS 2:11, 14–15

Our Lord Christ, we are humbled at the mystery of your resurrection and pray that you would draw us into your victorious life!

314

We are here to witness. . . . We can stage our own act on the planet—build our cities on its plains, dam its rivers, plant its topsoils—but our meaningful activity scarcely covers the terrain. We do not use songbirds, for instance. We do not eat many of them; we cannot befriend them; we cannot persuade them to eat more mosquitoes or plant fewer weed seeds. We can only witness them—whoever they are. If we were not here, they would be songbirds falling in the forest. If we were not here, material events like the passage of seasons would lack even the meager meanings we are able to muster for them. The show would play to an empty house.

TEACHING A STONE TO TALK BY ANNIE DILLARD, 1982

What profit is there in my death,
    if I go down to the Pit?
Will the dust praise you?
    Will it tell of your faithfulness?

PSALM 30:9

Lord our God, we thank you that you saw fit to place us as witnesses in the world, to give us eyes to notice a beautiful thing and ears to hear a bird's song.

315

Our God, Heaven cannot hold Him
Nor the earth sustain;
Heaven and earth shall flee away
When He comes to reign:
In the bleak midwinter
A stable-place sufficed
The Lord God Almighty
Jesus Christ.

FROM "A CHRISTMAS CAROL"
BY CHRISTINA ROSSETTI, 1872

And she gave birth to her firstborn son and wrapped him in bands of cloth, and laid him in a manger, because there was no place for them in the inn.

LUKE 2:7

O Christ, we praise you that you came in meekness, in poverty, and in love, our humble, fragile, infant God with Us.

316

A principal fruit of friendship is the ease and discharge of the fulness and swellings of the heart, which passions of all kinds do cause and induce. We know diseases of stoppings and suffocations are the most dangerous in the body; and it is not much otherwise in the mind . . . no receipt openeth the heart, but a true friend; to whom you may impart griefs, joys, fears, hopes, suspicions, counsels, and whatsoever lieth upon the heart to oppress it, in a kind of civil shrift or confession.

"OF FRIENDSHIP" BY FRANCIS BACON, 1612

A friend loves at all times,
and kinsfolk are born to share adversity.

PROVERBS 17:17

Our Lord, we give thanks to you for the many friends and loved ones you have placed in our lives. Thank you for the communion we share, the comfort we receive, and for the love that finds its source in you.

317

H e began praying quietly, but he soon felt that he was praying almost mechanically. Fragments of thought floated through his soul, flashed like stars, and went out again at once, to be succeeded by others. Yet there was reigning in his soul a sense of the wholeness of things—something steadfast and comforting—and he was aware of it himself. Sometimes he began praying ardently; he longed to pour out his thankfulness and love. . . . But when he had begun to pray, he passed suddenly to something else and sank into thought, forgetting both the prayer and what had interrupted it.

THE BROTHERS KARAMAZOV BY FYODOR DOSTOEVSKY, 1880

> Likewise the Spirit helps us in our weakness; for we do not know how to pray as we ought, but that very Spirit intercedes with sighs too deep for words.
>
> ROMANS 8:26

Holy Spirit, pray for us when we have no words, when drifting minds and tired bodies obscure our vision of God's kingdom.

318

The greatest thing a human soul ever does in this world is to *see* something, and tell what it *saw* in a plain way. Hundreds of people can talk for one who can think, but thousands can think for one who can see. To see clearly is poetry, prophecy, and religion,—all in one.

MODERN PAINTERS BY JOHN RUSKIN, 1843

I will pour out my spirit on all flesh;
your sons and daughters shall prophesy,
    your old men shall dream dreams,
    and your young men shall see visions.
Even on the male and female slaves,
    in those days, I will pour out my spirit.

JOEL 2:28-29

Holy God, give us eyes to see, truly, creatively, and with deep reverence and love.

319

---✦--- ❋ ---✦---

Simplicity, simplicity, simplicity! I say let your affairs be as two or three, and not a hundred or a thousand.

WALDEN BY HENRY DAVID THOREAU, 1854

But we urge you, beloved, to do so more and more, to aspire to live quietly, to mind your own affairs, and to work with your hands, as we directed you, so that you may behave properly toward outsiders and be dependent on no one.

1 THESSALONIANS 4:10B-12

Lord God, help us focus our minds on the things that truly matter, and not on the constant activity and motion of the world around us.

320

The Bible leaves no doubt at all about the sanctity of the act of world-making, or of the world that was made, or of creaturely or bodily life in this world. We are holy creatures living among other holy creatures in a world that is holy. Some people know this, and some do not. Nobody, of course, knows it all the time. But what keeps it from being far better known than it is? Why is it apparently unknown to millions of professed students of the Bible? How can modern Christianity have so solemnly folded its hands while so much of the work of God was and is being destroyed?

"CHRISTIANITY AND THE SURVIVAL OF CREATION" BY WENDELL BERRY, 1992

For every wild animal of the forest is mine,
    the cattle on a thousand hills.
I know all the birds of the air,
    and all that moves in the field is mine.

PSALM 50:10–11

Holy Lord, forgive us for the ways in which we are thoughtless and neglectful of the world around us. Forgive us our greed that sees the world as something to be used for our own gain, instead of as a gift to be cared for.

321

Had I realized at the time that for Austerlitz certain moments had no beginning or end, while on the other hand his whole life had sometimes seemed to him a blank point without duration, I would probably have waited more patiently.

AUSTERLITZ BY W. G. SEBALD, 2001

And we urge you, beloved, . . . encourage the fainthearted, help the weak, be patient with all of them.

1 THESSALONIANS 5:14

Our Father, give us compassion and attentive love to those around us, so that their hurts and longings won't go unnoticed.

322

It came over him now that the unexpected favors of fortune, no matter how dazzling, do not mean very much to us. They may excite or divert us for a time, but when we look back, the only things we cherish are those which in some way met our original want; the desire which formed in us in early youth, undirected, and of its own accord.

THE SONG OF THE LARK BY WILLA CATHER, 1915

Trust in the LORD, and do good;
    so you will live in the land, and enjoy security.
Take delight in the LORD,
    and he will give you the desires of your heart.

PSALM 37:3-4

Grant us, O Lord, those things that are most in accord with your will for us, and not the transitory pleasures we may believe we desire.

323

Thou art indeed just, Lord, if I contend
    With thee; but, sir, so what I plead is just.
Why do sinners' ways prosper? And why must
Disappointment all I endeavour end?

FROM "THOU ART INDEED JUST, LORD"
BY GERARD MANLEY HOPKINS, 1889

You will be in the right, O LORD,
    when I lay charges against you;
    but let me put my case to you.
Why does the way of the guilty prosper?
    Why do all who are treacherous thrive?

JEREMIAH 12:1

*Our Lord God, it is hard to see harm come to the weak and
oppressed, while comfort and luxury come to the oppressing and
powerful. We call to you for your justice, asking that we would
be brave enough to play a part in bringing it to bear on the
world's injustices.*

324

As I get considerably beyond the biblical allotment of three score years and ten, I feel with increasing intensity that I can express my gratitude for still being around on the oxygen-side of the earth's crust only by not standing pat on what I have hitherto known and loved. While oxygen lasts, there are still new things to love, especially if compassion is a form of love.

YOUNG MEN AND FIRE BY NORMAN MACLEAN, 1972

Listen to me, O house of Jacob,
   all the remnant of the house of Israel,
who have been borne by me from your birth,
   carried from the womb;
even to your old age I am he,
   even when you turn gray I will carry you.
I have made, and I will bear;
   I will carry and will save.

ISAIAH 46:3-4

As we age, God, help us to grow in wisdom and compassion; carry us and save us, we pray.

325

—※—

The Son of glory came down, and was slain,
   Us whom He had made, and Satan stol'n, to unbind.
'Twas much, that man was made like God before,
But that God should be made like man, much more.

FROM HOLY SONNET XV, "WILT THOU
LOVE GOD," BY JOHN DONNE, 1633

Let the same mind be in you that was in Christ Jesus,
   who, though he was in the form of God,
      did not regard equality with God
      as something to be exploited,
   but emptied himself,
      taking the form of a slave,
      being born in human likeness.

PHILIPPIANS 2:5–7A

*Lord Christ, God with Us, we sit in awe of your incarnation, of
your life of love brought to meet us in our weakness.*

326

A ripple of wind comes down from the woods and across the clearing toward us. We see a wave of shadow and gloss where the short grass bends and the cottage eaves tremble. It hits us in the back. It is a single gust, a sport, a rogue breeze out of the north, as if some reckless, impatient wind has bumped the north door open on its hinges and let out this acre of scent familiar and forgotten, this cool scent of tundra, and of November. Fall! Who authorized this intrusion? . . . It is an entirely misplaced air—fall, that I have utterly forgotten, that could be here again, another fall, and here it is only July. I thought I was younger, and would have more time.

TEACHING A STONE TO TALK BY ANNIE DILLARD, 1982

You have made my days a few handbreadths,
   and my lifetime is as nothing in your sight.
Surely everyone stands as a mere breath.

PSALM 39:5

Lord of all creation, as we marvel or fear or simply witness the passage of time, give us affection and attention for the unfolding of our miraculous lives.

327

-:——※——:-

A story was something you made up out of something that might have happened. Only you didn't tell it like it was, you told it like you thought it should have been.

A TREE GROWS IN BROOKLYN BY BETTY SMITH, 1943

For this reason it depends on faith, in order that the promise may rest on grace and be guaranteed to all his descendants, not only to the adherents of the law but also to those who share the faith of Abraham (for he is the father of all of us, as it is written, "I have made you the father of many nations")—in the presence of the God in whom he believed, who gives life to the dead and calls into existence the things that do not exist.

ROMANS 4:16-17

Our Lord and our God, we praise you for your new, old story of transformation, forgiveness, and renewal!

328

If personality is an unbroken series of successful gestures, then there was something gorgeous about him, some heightened sensitivity to the promises of life, as if he were related to one of those intricate machines that register earthquakes ten thousand miles away. . . . it was an extraordinary gift for hope, a romantic readiness such as I have never found in any other person and which it is not likely I shall ever find again.

THE GREAT GATSBY BY F. SCOTT FITZGERALD, 1925

Keep alert, stand firm in your faith, be courageous, be strong. Let all that you do be done in love.

1 CORINTHIANS 16:13-14

God, heighten our awareness of those around us, that we may be present and able to show love wherever it is needed.

329

M y heart be brave, and do not falter so,
  Nor utter more that deep, despairing wail.
Thy way is very dark and drear I know,
But do not let thy strength and courage fail;
For certain as the raven-winged night
Is followed by the bright and blushing morn,
Thy coming morrow will be clear and bright;
'Tis darkest when the night is furthest worn.
Look up, and out, beyond, surrounding clouds,
And do not in thine own gross darkness grope,
Rise up, and casting off thy hind'ring shrouds,
Cling thou to this, and ever inspiring hope:
Tho' thick the battle and tho' fierce the fight,
There is a power making for the right.

"SONNET" BY JAMES WELDON JOHNSON, 1917

Let us know, let us press on to know the LORD;
    his appearing is as sure as the dawn;
he will come to us like the showers,
    like the spring rains that water the earth.

HOSEA 6:3

*Lord, you are the light in the darkness, our ever-present hope,
and we give thanks for you.*

330

Hatred, which could destroy so much, never failed to destroy the man who hated and this was an immutable law.

NOTES OF A NATIVE SON BY JAMES BALDWIN, 1955

We know that we have passed from death to life because we love one another. Whoever does not love abides in death. All who hate a brother or sister are murderers, and you know that murderers do not have eternal life abiding in them. We know love by this, that he laid down his life for us—and we ought to lay down our lives for one another. How does God's love abide in anyone who has the world's goods and sees a brother or sister in need and yet refuses help?

1 JOHN 3:14–17

Lord, it is easier sometimes to hate than to love, but we know this is not your commandment, and we know it destroys us in the process. Help us to love each other, to respect each other, and to realize how much we need each other.

331

The weight of this sad time we must obey,
   Speak what we feel, not what we ought to say.
The oldest have borne most; we that are young
Shall never see so much, nor live so long.

KING LEAR BY WILLIAM SHAKESPEARE, 1606

I pour out my complaint before him;
   I tell my trouble before him.
When my spirit is faint,
   you know my way.

PSALM 142:2–3

God, you know that at times this world breaks our hearts. Grant us peace and courage that we might comfort others and be ourselves comforted.

332

Differences of habit and language are nothing at all if our aims are identical and our hearts are open.

HARRY POTTER AND THE GOBLET OF FIRE BY J. K. ROWLING, 2000

For in Christ Jesus you are all children of God through faith. As many of you as were baptized into Christ have clothed yourselves with Christ. There is no longer Jew or Greek, there is no longer slave or free, there is no longer male and female; for all of you are one in Christ Jesus. And if you belong to Christ, then you are Abraham's offspring, heirs according to the promise.

GALATIANS 3:26–29

Lord of all the nations, help us to know that in our diversity is our strength, and to keep our hearts ever open to each other in love and service.

333

─┤─────※─────┤─

If you look for perfection, you'll never be content.

ANNA KARENINA BY LEO TOLSTOY, 1877

If we say that we have no sin, we deceive ourselves, and the truth is not in us. If we confess our sins, he who is faithful and just will forgive us our sins and cleanse us from all unrighteousness.

1 JOHN 1:8–9

Holy God, free us from the burden of perfectionism, and may we find our identity in you and in your daily forgiveness.

334

By then I wasn't just asking questions; I was being changed by them. I was being changed by my prayers, which dwindled down nearer and nearer to silence, which weren't confrontations with God but with the difficulty—in my own mind, or in the human lot—of knowing what or how to pray. Lying awake at night, I could feel myself being changed—into what, I had no idea.

JAYBER CROW BY WENDELL BERRY, 2000

The LORD is near to all who call on him,
    to all who call on him in truth.
He fulfills the desire of all who fear him;
    he also hears their cry, and saves them.

PSALM 145:18–19

Lord, when we wonder about the efficacy or purpose of our prayers, remind us that while things outside may seem the same, inside we are being transformed.

335

Vanity and pride are different things, though the words are often used synonymously. A person may be proud without being vain. Pride relates more to our opinion of ourselves, vanity to what we would have others think of us.

PRIDE AND PREJUDICE BY JANE AUSTEN, 1813

Do nothing from selfish ambition or conceit, but in humility regard others as better than yourselves.

PHILIPPIANS 2:3

Father of all, give us eyes to see that we are all individuals created by you. Set us free from seeking our identity through the approval of others. May we know we are all beloved.

336

It's a good thing when a man is different from your image of him. It shows he isn't a type. If he were, it would be the end of him as a man. But if you can't place him in a category, it means that at least a part of him is what a human being ought to be.

DOCTOR ZHIVAGO BY BORIS PASTERNAK, 1957

Honor everyone. Love the family of believers. Fear God.

1 PETER 2:17

Holy Lord, help us to truly see those around us and to honor each individual as one who bears your image.

337

—✛——※——✛—

"Lady," he said, and turned and gave her his full attention, "lemme tell you something. There's one of these doctors in Atlanta that's taken a knife and cut the human heart—the human heart," he repeated, leaning forward, "out of a man's chest and held it in his hand," and he held his hand out, palm up, as if it were slightly weighted with the human heart, "and studied it like it was a day-old chicken, and lady," he said, allowing a long significant pause in which his head slid forward and his clay-colored eyes brightened, "he don't know no more about it than you or me."

"THE LIFE YOU SAVE MAY BE YOUR OWN"
BY FLANNERY O'CONNOR, 1955

When I look at your heavens, the work of your fingers,
   the moon and the stars that you have established;
what are human beings that you are mindful of them,
   mortals that you care for them?

PSALM 8:3-4

Lord, beyond all that we can comprehend or imagine you to be, we are humbled that you would care for us in all our fragility and weakness.

338

<hr/>

It was when he said expansively *There is*
no such thing as the truth that his thick thumbs
thickened and his lips, purple as grapes,
further purpled.

FROM "ANOTHER ROAD HOME"
BY SCOTT CAIRNS, 2014

Pilate asked him, "So you are a king?" Jesus answered, "You say that I am a king. For this I was born, and for this I came into the world, to testify to the truth. Everyone who belongs to the truth listens to my voice." Pilate asked him, "What is truth?"

JOHN 18:37-38

God of Truth, help us to know and act on what is real and lasting in this life, to discard our illusions, and to serve only the truth.

339

I break your bonds and masterships,
And I unchain the slave:
Free be his heart and hand henceforth
As wind and wandering wave.

FROM "BOSTON HYMN" BY
RALPH WALDO EMERSON, 1863

Then they cried to the LORD in their trouble,
and he saved them from their distress;
he brought them out of darkness and gloom,
and broke their bonds asunder.

PSALM 107:13–14

*Christ our Lord, bring your freedom to those held in bondage
of mind, spirit, or body.*

340

Things had happened to her that were hers alone, and had nothing to do with them. It was the first time. And no amount of telling about it could help them understand or share what she felt. It was satisfying and lonely, both at once.

TUCK EVERLASTING BY NATALIE BABBITT, 1975

O Lord, all my longing is known to you;
my sighing is not hidden from you.

PSALM 38:9

Our Lord, you see all our longings, and know the desires of our hearts. Give us the courage to pursue the desires you have placed in us, even when they are not recognized or respected by others.

341

Then you must teach my daughter this same lesson. How to lose your innocence but not your hope. How to laugh forever.

THE JOY LUCK CLUB BY AMY TAN, 1989

At that time the disciples came to Jesus and asked, "Who is the greatest in the kingdom of heaven?" He called a child, whom he put among them, and said, "Truly I tell you, unless you change and become like children, you will never enter the kingdom of heaven."

MATTHEW 18:1–3

As with the innocence of children, Lord Christ, you called us to you. Teach us anew how you would have us approach your throne.

342

I went around saying for a long time that I am not one of those Christians who is heavily into forgiveness—that I am one of the other kind. But even though it was funny, and actually true, it started to be too painful to stay this way. They say we are not punished for the sin but by the sin, and I began to feel punished by my unwillingness to forgive.

TRAVELING MERCIES: SOME THOUGHTS ON FAITH BY ANNE LAMOTT, 1999

You have heard that it was said to those of ancient times, "You shall not murder"; and "whoever murders shall be liable to judgment." But I say to you that if you are angry with a brother or sister, you will be liable to judgment; and if you insult a brother or sister, you will be liable to the council; and if you say, "You fool," you will be liable to the hell of fire. So when you are offering your gift at the altar, if you remember that your brother or sister has something against you, leave your gift there before the altar and go; first be reconciled to your brother or sister, and then come and offer your gift.

MATTHEW 5:21–24

Lord, you forgive before we even ask; help us to extend something like that same grace to other children of God, and to always be aware that failing to forgive distances us from you, from each other, and from ourselves.

343

Pet names are a persistent remnant of childhood, a reminder that life is not always so serious, so formal, so complicated. They are a reminder, too, that one is not all things to all people.

THE NAMESAKE BY JHUMPA LAHIRI, 2003

Then he took a little child and put it among them; and taking it in his arms, he said to them, "Whoever welcomes one such child in my name welcomes me, and whoever welcomes me welcomes not me but the one who sent me."

MARK 9:36–37

Heavenly Parent, help us to see ourselves the way you see us, as your beloved children, to feel confident in your affection through all our lives.

344

When I left Queen's my future seemed to stretch out before me like a straight road. I thought I could see along it for many a milestone. Now there is a bend in it. I don't know what lies around the bend, but I'm going to believe that the best does. I wonder how the road beyond it goes—what there is of green glory and soft, checkered light and shadows—what new land-scapes—what new beauties—what curves and hills and valleys further on.

ANNE OF GREEN GABLES BY LUCY MAUD MONTGOMERY, 1908

For surely I know the plans I have for you, says the LORD, plans for your welfare and not for harm, to give you a future with hope.

JEREMIAH 29:11

Help me, Lord, to know that in you, no matter where I am or how I feel, I am never lost, never hopeless, never outside of your love or your plans for me.

345

In the open air alone I found relief; among nature's beauteous works, her God reassumed his attribute of benevolence, and again I could trust that he who built up the mountains, planted the forest, and poured out the rivers, would erect another state for lost humanity, where we might awaken again to our affections, our happiness, and our faith.

THE LAST MAN BY MARY SHELLEY, 1826

Thus says the LORD:
Heaven is my throne
   and the earth is my footstool;
what is the house that you would build for me,
   and what is my resting place?
All these things my hand has made,
   and so all these things are mine,

                says the LORD.

ISAIAH 66:1-2A

Holy Lord, in view of the vast and varied world, we are humbled at our small place in it. Thank you that while you don't need us, still your heart is filled with abundant love for us.

346

Oh, for the wonder that bubbles into my soul,
I would be a good fountain, a good well-head,
Would blur no whisper, spoil no expression.

What is the knocking?
What is the knocking at the door in the night?
It is somebody wants to do us harm.

No, no, it is the three strange angels.
Admit them, admit them.

FROM "SONG OF A MAN WHO HAS COME
THROUGH" BY D. H. LAWRENCE, 1917

Let mutual love continue. Do not neglect to show hospitality to strangers, for by doing that some have entertained angels without knowing it.

HEBREWS 13:1–2

Lord God who welcomes me, may my heart be open, attentive, and inclined toward all around me, known or unknown.

347

People talk about the courage of condemned men walking to the place of execution: sometimes it needs as much courage to walk with any kind of bearing towards another person's habitual misery.

THE HEART OF THE MATTER BY GRAHAM GREENE, 1948

Hope deferred makes the heart sick,
  but a desire fulfilled is a tree of life.

PROVERBS 13:12

Grant us strength and courage, Lord, to take on the trials and tribulations of this life, and grant us the compassion to love and serve those suffering more than ourselves.

348

My silk heart's
    filled with lights,
lost bells,
lilies and bees,
and I'll go far,
further than these mountains,
further than the seas,
close to the stars
and I'll say to Christ,
Lord, give me back
the child's soul I once had,
steeped in legends,
with the feathered cap
and the wooden sabre.

FROM "BALLAD OF THE
LITTLE SQUARE" BY
FEDERICO GARCÍA LORCA, 1921

But Jesus said, "Let the little children come to me, and do
not stop them; for it is to such as these that the kingdom
of heaven belongs."

MATTHEW 19:14

*Make us like little children again, Lord, that we may draw near
to the kingdom of heaven.*

349

He wondered if any in all the hurrying crowd had come from such a house of mourning. He thought they all looked joyous, and he was angry with them. But he could not, you cannot, read the lot of those who daily pass you by in the street. How do you know the wild romances of their lives; the trials, the temptations they are even now enduring, resisting, sinking under?

MARY BARTON BY ELIZABETH GASKELL, 1848

Do not judge, and you will not be judged; do not condemn, and you will not be condemned. Forgive, and you will be forgiven.

LUKE 6:37

In every life, we know, Lord, there are secret heartbreaks and unknown difficulties. Walk with us in our own hard times, we pray, and help us to walk with others, loving without judging.

350

"Monseigneur, you are always anxious to make everything useful, but yet here is a plate that is of no use. It would be much better to have salads there than bouquets."

"Madame Magloire," replied the Bishop, "you are mistaken. The beautiful is as useful as the useful." He added, after a moment's silence, "perhaps more so."

LES MISÉRABLES BY VICTOR HUGO, 1862

Let the heavens be glad, and let the earth rejoice;
     let the sea roar, and all that fills it;
     let the field exult, and everything in it.
Then shall all the trees of the forest sing for joy
     before the LORD.

PSALM 96:11–13A

Lord of all the earth, we praise you for the world of beauty that surrounds us, and for what it reveals to us about your delight and affection for all you have made.

351

The only God who seems to me to be worth believing in is impossible for mortal man to understand, and therefore he teaches us through this impossible. But we rebel against the impossible. I sense a wish in some professional religion-mongers to make God possible, to make him comprehensible to the naked intellect, domesticate him so that he's easy to believe in. Every century the Church makes a fresh attempt to make Christianity acceptable. But an acceptable Christianity is not Christian; a comprehensible God is no more than an idol. I don't want that kind of God.

THE IRRATIONAL SEASON BY MADELEINE L'ENGLE, 1977

> But will God indeed reside with mortals on earth? Even heaven and the highest heaven cannot contain you, how much less this house that I have built!
>
> 2 CHRONICLES 6:18

Holy God, forgive us for making you smaller than you are, and may we be humble enough to sit with your mystery.

352

If I write something, I fear it will happen, and if I love too much, I fear I will lose that person; nevertheless, I cannot stop writing or loving.

PAULA BY ISABEL ALLENDE, 1994

For God did not give us a spirit of cowardice, but rather a spirit of power and of love and of self-discipline.

2 TIMOTHY 1:7

God, you have given us gifts to serve you. Let us never shrink away from offering them to you and to the world.

353

The gold had kept his thoughts in an ever-repeated circle, leading to nothing beyond itself; but Eppie was an object compacted of changes and hopes that forced his thoughts onward, and carried them . . . away to the new things that would come with the coming years . . . reawakening his senses with her fresh life, even to the old winter-flies that came crawling forth in the early spring sunshine, and warming him into joy because *she* had joy.

SILAS MARNER BY GEORGE ELIOT, 1861

You have turned my mourning into dancing;
　　you have taken off my sackcloth
　　and clothed me with joy,
so that my soul may praise you and not be silent.
　　O LORD my God, I will give thanks to you forever.

PSALM 30:11–12

Our Lord, give us eyes to see the beauties and joys of the world around us!

354

The land belongs to the future, Carl; that's the way it seems to me. How many of the names on the country clerk's plat will be there in fifty years? I might as well try to will the sunset over there to my brother's children. We come and go, but the land is always here. And the people who love it and understand it are the people who own it—for a little while.

O PIONEERS! BY WILLA CATHER, 1913

The heavens are yours, the earth also is yours;
   the world and all that is in it—you have founded them.

PSALM 89:11

Give us a respect and reverence, Lord, for your creation, that we might see you in it and through it.

355

I am sure I have always thought of Christmas time, when it has come round . . . as a good time; a kind, forgiving, charitable, pleasant time; the only time I know of, in the long calendar of the year, when men and women seem by one consent to open their shut-up hearts freely, and to think of people below them as if they really were fellow-passengers to the grave, and not another race of creatures bound on other journeys.

A CHRISTMAS CAROL BY CHARLES DICKENS, 1843

But the angel said to them, "Do not be afraid; for see—I am bringing you good news of great joy for all the people: to you is born this day in the city of David a Savior, who is the Messiah, the Lord."

LUKE 2:10-11

O infant Christ, we praise you for coming as our great joy, as a gift to all people.

356

The very good people did not convince me; I felt they'd never been tempted. But you knew; you understood; you felt the world outside tugging at one with all its golden hands—and you hated the things it asked of one; you hated happiness bought by disloyalty and cruelty and indifference. That was what I'd never known before—and it's better than anything I've known.

THE AGE OF INNOCENCE BY EDITH WHARTON, 1920

For we do not have a high priest who is unable to sympathize with our weaknesses, but we have one who in every respect has been tested as we are, yet without sin. Let us therefore approach the throne of grace with boldness, so that we may receive mercy and find grace to help in time of need.

HEBREWS 4:15-16

God, you know us, you want the best for us, and you offer us blessings beyond our reckoning. Help us to recognize them and accept them.

357

Take of this grain, which in my garden grows
       And grows for you;
Make bread of it: and that repose
    And peace which ev'ry where
With so much earnestnesse you do pursue,
    Is onely there.

FROM "PEACE" BY GEORGE HERBERT, 1633

Peace I leave with you; my peace I give to you. I do not give to you as the world gives. Do not let your hearts be troubled, and do not let them be afraid.

JOHN 14:27

Prince of Peace, free us from the fear that makes us set guards around our lives, and lead us into that wide peace which we cannot make for ourselves.

358

To die, it's easy. But you have to struggle for life.

MAUS I: A SURVIVOR'S TALE; MY FATHER
BLEEDS HISTORY BY ART SPIEGELMAN, 1991

For it was you who formed my inward parts;
    you knit me together in my mother's womb.
I praise you, for I am fearfully and wonderfully made.
    Wonderful are your works;
that I know very well.

PSALM 139:13–14

Gracious God, we thank you for the gift of life. Give us the
strength and courage to live completely, that we may serve you
faithfully.

359

Doesn't everything die at last, and too soon?
Tell me, what is it you plan to do
with your one wild and precious life?

FROM "THE SUMMER DAY" BY
MARY OLIVER, 1990

But those who wait for the LORD shall renew their strength,
   they shall mount up with wings like eagles,
they shall run and not be weary,
   they shall walk and not faint.

ISAIAH 40:31

*This life you have given us is precious, Lord. Grant us the
strength to live it to the fullest, and to live for the things that
truly matter.*

360

S he would only point out the salvation that was latent in his own soul, and in the soul of every man. Only connect! That was the whole of her sermon. Only connect the prose and the passion, and both will be exalted, and human love will be seen at its height. Live in fragments no longer.

HOWARD'S END BY E. M. FORSTER, 1910

The gifts he gave were that some would be apostles, some prophets, some evangelists, some pastors and teachers, to equip the saints for the work of ministry, for building up the body of Christ, until all of us come to the unity of the faith and of the knowledge of the Son of God, to maturity, to the measure of the full stature of Christ. We must no longer be children, tossed to and fro and blown about by every wind of doctrine, by people's trickery, by their craftiness in deceitful scheming. But speaking the truth in love, we must grow up in every way into him who is the head, into Christ, from whom the whole body, joined and knit together by every ligament with which it is equipped, as each part is working properly, promotes the body's growth in building itself up in love.

EPHESIANS 4:11-16

Holy God, we ask you to work your healing in the places where our lives are fragmented, and to bring us into communion with those around us.

361

Your mother died to save you. If there is one thing Volde-mort cannot understand, it is love. Love as powerful as your mother's for you leaves its own mark. To have been loved so deeply, even though the person who loved us is gone, will give us some protection forever.

HARRY POTTER AND THE SORCERER'S
STONE BY J. K. ROWLING, 1997

For I received from the Lord what I also handed on to you, that the Lord Jesus on the night when he was betrayed took a loaf of bread, and when he had given thanks, he broke it and said, "This is my body that is for you. Do this in remembrance of me." In the same way he took the cup also, after supper, saying, "This cup is the new covenant in my blood. Do this, as often as you drink it, in remem-brance of me." For as often as you eat this bread and drink the cup, you proclaim the Lord's death until he comes.

1 CORINTHIANS 11:23-26

Holy Christ, in your sacrifice we are made whole, and in your love, we are made complete. Thank you for loving us so deeply.

362

The man had to touch him twice on the shoulder before he woke, and as he opened his eyes a faint smile passed across his lips, as though he had been lost in some delightful dream. Yet he had not dreamed at all. His night had been untroubled by any images of pleasure or of pain. But youth smiles without any reason. It is one of its chiefest charms.

THE PICTURE OF DORIAN GRAY BY OSCAR WILDE, 1890

Rejoice always.

1 THESSALONIANS 5:16

Lord Christ, fill our hearts with joy as we remember your story of love and redemption!

363

How poor are they that have not patience! What wound did ever heal but by degrees?

OTHELLO BY WILLIAM SHAKESPEARE, 1604

Commit your way to the LORD;
  trust in him, and he will act.
He will make your vindication shine like the light,
  and the justice of your cause like the noonday.

Be still before the LORD, and wait patiently for him.

PSALM 37:5–7A

O God, it is hard to be patient, to wait for healing when we don't feel certain of its arrival. Help us.

364

Eventually, all things merge into one, and a river runs through it. The river was cut by the world's great flood and runs over rocks from the basement of time. On some of the rocks are timeless raindrops. Under the rocks are the words, and some of the words are theirs.

A RIVER RUNS THROUGH IT AND OTHER STORIES BY NORMAN MACLEAN, 1976

In the beginning was the Word, and the Word was with God, and the Word was God. He was in the beginning with God. All things came into being through him, and without him not one thing came into being. What has come into being in him was life, and the life was the light of all people. The light shines in the darkness, and the darkness did not overcome it.

JOHN 1:1–5

O Word of Life, speak to us. Call us, comfort us, and remind us that since the beginning of time, you have loved us.

365

We shall not cease from exploration
And the end of all our exploring
Will be to arrive where we started
And know the place for the first time.

FROM "LITTLE GIDDING"
BY T. S. ELIOT, 1942

Thus you shall salute him: "Peace be to you, and peace be to your house, and peace be to all that you have."

1 SAMUEL 25:6

Holy One, bring us home at last in peace to know, love, and serve you.

Afterword

Every year—sometimes more than once—I teach a class, lead a retreat, or offer a session for priests, pastors, or seminarians on how and why people of faith read great literature. In the course of a weekend or longer, we discuss poetry and short fiction, drama and film, novels, essays and spiritual autobiography, and in the process, we explore both the pragmatic and the spiritual value of great literary works. These folks with whom I'm working, especially if they're doing parish ministry or are preparing to, are thinking practically about the work pastors do in the pulpit, and we do acknowledge that great preachers often read voraciously, seeking stories and illustrations. Practical too is the attention to craft, what we can learn from great writers about sound, language, image, rhythm, characterization for the preaching event. But the greatest part of why I lead these sessions—and the greater part of why for over three decades I myself have been so engaged in telling my own stories, reading those of others, and reflecting on both—is the personal formation that we experience from great literature. Whether the writers are people of faith or not (as much as I love the Christian writers Flannery O'Connor and Walker Percy and the Christian rock band U2, I often speak about how filmmaker Quentin Tarantino's work has been life-changing for me, despite the fact that nobody seems to be claiming him for their faith traditions), these works wrestle with the Big Questions, often with grace and humor and beauty that we don't find in our everyday lives.

In those literature and preaching conversations, and in most of the other kinds of speaking I do, I've found we often end up talking about some story or poem or novel or song that has changed our lives—or saved them. I know from my own history that there are novels and movies and images from poetry that came into my life at precisely the moment I needed them most, whether to get me through a really hard day or to help me understand something about existence that had eluded me up to that point. Great literature has shaped and formed me, and I'm sure you also have similar stories. Part of why we are the way we are, if we are readers, is because of what we have read.

In fact, the only thing remotely close to the transformative experience we get from literature comes from another (some might say The) Great Book, the Bible. Set aside for just a moment the question of whether or not the Bible is sacred (or how it is, perhaps). In these powerful stories and beautiful poems inspired by God, we get more wrestling with the Big Questions, often in the form of really messy human lives, which are the lives with which I most identify. The struggles and faith of Abraham and Sarah, of Jacob, of Joseph, of David, of the Blessed Virgin Mary, of the imperfect disciples of Jesus, of Mary Magdalene, of Paul also speak into my life every day, and the pairing of great literature and the Scriptures was one of the appealing ideas behind this project when my friends at Westminster John Knox proposed it.

The other appealing thing about doing this collection was that I would be working with the writer and editor Sabrina Fountain, who, providentially, had been assigned to be my research assistant at Baylor University in the fall of 2018. I had taught Sabrina in a graduate writing workshop, had read her wondrous nonfiction, and knew that in her, I had the perfect partner for the book that WJK envisioned. I want to be clear: Sabrina's hard work made this book possible, and her beautiful foreword and many hours spent compiling quotations are the backbone of this work. I would and could not have taken it on without her.

As you've read (I hope) in that foreword, Sabrina, like me, believes that something powerful, meaningful, and (dare we say it?) sacred takes place in great art. Augustine believed that in the pagan literature he consumed before becoming Christian he was actually being drawn closer to God, secular though that literature might be deemed to be, and he concluded in *On Christian Doctrine* that whatever is true and beautiful is of the Lord. In similar fashion, in an extended conversation for publication last summer, Rowan Williams and I talked about how sacred and secular literature are often doing the same thing, and I love the way Rowan formulated what happens when great writers take on the Big Questions: "When human beings are to some degree opened up by pain, by love, by compassion, by dread, by any number of things, what they're opening to is that More than You Thought, which is at the heart of the world, and that More than You Thought opens ultimately onto the energy of God."[1] As Augustine argued—and experienced himself—the work of thoughtful and sensitive writers opens onto the energy of God.

So, coming back to that question we momentarily set aside, I do believe that the Bible is sacred, but I also believe that in a not dissimilar way, the great creations of human beings made

---

1. Rowan Williams and Greg Garrett, *In Conversation: Rowan Williams and Greg Garrett* (New York: Church Publishing, 2019), 84.

in the image of a creator God are sacred. In this book, you have the opportunity to see those two instances of the sacred rub up against each other, strike sparks, and, I hope, open your eyes to that More than You Thought of which Rowan spoke.

A few notes on the way Sabrina and I worked: First, we came to the construction of this book entirely through the literary passages we chose (and the consideration of many more we didn't). Our goal was to select wildly diverse writers who spoke to the whole range of human emotions and difficulties—that pain, love, compassion, dread, and other things we just mentioned—and I think we accomplished that. Clearly there are some writers to whom we are strongly drawn—I suspect that Sabrina, the essayist, could have populated an entire devotional book with quotations from Wendell Berry and other great essay writers, just as I kept coming back to my favorites: Anne Lamott, James Baldwin, J. K. Rowling, and Marilynne Robinson.

It was of course Marilynne Robinson's luminescent words from near the end of *Gilead* that we chose for the title of our book, and I love how that particular passage actually captures the idea we've been exploring here that God reveals God's self to us through more than just Holy Scripture if we are open to how God might be moving in the world, if we only have the courage (as Robinson's John Ames says) to see. Those passages we selected lit up the world for us in a powerful way, and I hope you too will discover new writers and rediscover familiar ones through this process of reading for wisdom.

After we had chosen passages, we then paired them with Scripture that either echoed the literary selection or sang a countermelody to it. We very consciously did not begin by selecting Scripture, which means that we did not choose based on some theological agenda, although I think you'll note how widely we ranged in using Scripture, ultimately choosing verses from almost every book in the Bible. That was, however, a happy accident (or, again, perhaps, providential). You'll note that we did tend to lean heavily on the Wisdom literature, as is perhaps only logical for a book full of literary selections exploring the human condition, but you'll also find us citing everything from Habukkuk to tiny Titus.

Sabrina and I have probably demonstrated our personal theological biases in these choices, since our passions for beauty, compassion, and justice do seem to be conspicuous. But we also tried to be responsive to the variety of ways that Tolstoy and Toni Morrison and Shakespeare, that *The Brothers Karamazov* and *Jane Eyre* and *Gilead* open up the human condition— including our pettiness, selfishness, and brokenness. I trust that any person reading through the entire book will feel that we have properly represented the many facets of faith and wisdom.

Finally, we concluded each section with a prayer, again trying to respond to the melodies being sung in the literary passage and in the accompanying Scripture. As a preacher, I'm aware that anytime you're doing exegesis, anytime you interpret a text, there are multiple paths down which that text may lead you. These prayers, while, I hope, meaningful to you, are of course not the only prayers that these selections might evoke, and I hope you will add in your own prayers as you need and desire.

What you have in your hands—or on your screen—then, ultimately, is the work that Sabrina and I have curated for you, a selection of great literature, scriptural wisdom, and prayer that we hope will carry you through hard days and celebrate good ones, that will offer insight and inspiration, that will introduce

you to some new writers, and that will help you see the world—
and God—in fresh new ways. Thank you for reading. May it be
a blessing to you.

> "Let the favor of the Lord our God be upon us,
> and prosper for us the work of our hands—
> O prosper the work of our hands!"
>
> (Psalm 90:17)

Greg Garrett
Epiphany 2019
Austin, Texas

Bibliography

Alcott, Louisa May. *Little Women*. New York: Grossett & Dunlap, 1947.

Allende, Isabel. *The House of the Spirits*. Translated by Magda Bogin. New York: Atria Paperback, 2015.

———. *Paula*. Translated by Margaret Sayers Peden. New York: HarperPerennial, 1996.

Anaya, Rudolfo. *Bless Me, Ultima*. New York: Warner Books, 1994.

Angelou, Maya. *I Know Why the Caged Bird Sings*. New York: Random House, 2015.

———. "On the Pulse of Morning." In *On the Pulse of Morning*. New York: Random House, 1993.

Austen, Jane. *Emma*. New York: Barnes & Noble, 2003.

———. *Northanger Abbey*. London: Penguin Books, 2003.

———. *Pride and Prejudice*. London: Penguin Books, 2003.

———. *Sense and Sensibility*. London: Penguin Books, 2003.

Babbitt, Natalie. *Tuck Everlasting*. New York: Square Fish, 2007.

Bacon, Francis. "Of Friendship." In *Modern and Classical Essayists: Twelve Masters*. Mountain View, CA: Mayfield, 1996.

Baldwin, James. *The Fire Next Time*. New York: Vintage Books, 1993.

———. *I Am Not Your Negro*. New York: Vintage Books, 2017.

———. *Notes of a Native Son*. Boston: Beacon Press, 2012.

Bashō, Matsuo. *Narrow Road to the Interior and Other Writings*. Translated by Sam Hamill. Boston: Shambhala, 2006.

Berry, Wendell. "Christianity and the Survival of Creation." In *The Art of the Commonplace*. New York: Shoemaker & Hoard, 2002.

———. "The Gift of Good Land." In *The Art of the Commonplace*. New York: Shoemaker & Hoard, 2002.

———. *Jayber Crow*. Berkeley, CA: Counterpoint, 2000.

———. "The Pleasures of Eating." In *Bringing It to the Table: On Farming and Food*. Berkeley, CA: Counterpoint, 2009.

Bolaño, Roberto. *Last Evenings on Earth*. Translated by Chris Andrews. New York: New Directions Books, 2006.

Bonhoeffer, Dietrich. *Life Together*. Translated by John W. Doberstein. New York: HarperCollins, 1954.

Borges, Jorge Luis. *Jorge Luis Borges: Selected Non-Fictions*. Translated by Esther Allen, Suzanne Jill Levine, and Eliot Weinberger. New York: Penguin Books, 2000.

Brontë, Charlotte. *Jane Eyre*. New York: Vintage Books, 2009.

Browning, Elizabeth Barrett. "Love." In *Sonnets from the Portuguese*. New York: St. Martin's Press, 1986.

Buechner, Frederick. *Brendan*. New York: HarperCollins, 1987.

———. *Telling the Truth: The Gospel as Tragedy, Comedy, and Fairy Tale*. New York: HarperCollins, 1977.

Buonarroti, Michelangelo. *Sonnets: Michelangelo*. Translated by Elizabeth Jennings. New York: Routledge, 2002.

Burnett, Frances Hodgson. *A Little Princess*. London: Puffin Books, 2014.

———. *The Secret Garden*. New York: HarperCollins, 2010.

Cairns, Scott. *Slow Pilgrim: Collected Poems*. Brewster, MA: Paraclete Press, 2015.

Cather, Willa. *Death Comes for the Archbishop*. New York: Vintage Books, 1990.

———. *My Ántonia*. Boston: Houghton Mifflin, 1954.

———. *O Pioneers!* Oxford: Oxford University Press, 2008.

———. *The Professor's House*. New York: Vintage Books, 1990.

———. *The Song of the Lark*. New York: Vintage Books, 1990.

Chesterton, G. K. *The Ball and the Cross*. New York: Barnes & Noble, 2006.

Cisneros, Sandra. *The House on Mango Street*. New York: Vintage Books, 1991.

Coleridge, Mary Elizabeth. "After St. Augustine." In *The Oxford Book of English Mystical Verse*. Edited by D. H. S. Nicholson and A. H. E. Lee. Oxford: Oxford University Press, 1917.

Dickens, Charles. *A Christmas Carol*. New York: W. W. Norton, 2017.

———. *Great Expectations*. London: Penguin Books, 2003.

———. *A Tale of Two Cities*. Ware, UK: Wordsworth Editions, 1993.

Dickinson, Emily. "I Died for Beauty." In *The Complete Poems of Emily Dickinson*. Edited by Thomas H. Johnson. Boston: Back Bay Books, 1961.

Dillard, Annie. *Pilgrim at Tinker Creek*. New York: HarperPerennial, 2013.

———. *Teaching a Stone to Talk*. New York: HarperPerennial, 2013.

———. *The Writing Life*. New York: Harper & Row, 1989.

Donne, John. *John Donne: Holy Sonnets*. Newton, NJ: Vicarage Hill Press, 2014.

———. "Resurrection, Imperfect." In *John Donne: Selected Poetry*. Edited by Marius Bewley. New York: Signet Classics, 1966.

Dostoevsky, Fyodor. *The Adolescent*. Translated by Richard Pevear and Larissa Volokhonsky. New York: Vintage Books, 2003.

———. *The Brothers Karamazov*. Translated by Richard Pevear and Larissa Volokhonsky. New York: Alfred A. Knopf, 1990.

———. *Crime and Punishment*. Translated by Richard Pevear and Larissa Volokhonsky. New York: Vintage Books, 1993.

Douglass, Frederick. *Narrative of the Life of Frederick Douglass, An American Slave*. New York: Barnes & Noble, 2013.

Dumas, Alexandre. *The Count of Monte Cristo*. Translated by Robin Buss. London: Penguin Books, 2003.

Dunbar, Paul Laurence. *Paul Laurence Dunbar: Selected Poems*. Edited by Glenn Mott. Mineola, NY: Dover Publications, 1997.

Eliot, George. *Adam Bede*. Oxford: Oxford University Press, 2008.

———. *Middlemarch*. London: Penguin Books, 2003.

———. *The Mill on the Floss*. London: Penguin Books, 2003.

———. *Silas Marner*. Oxford: Oxford University Press, 2017.

Eliot, T. S. "Little Gidding." In *Four Quartets*. San Diego, CA: Harcourt, Brace, 1971.

Ellison, Ralph. *Invisible Man*. New York: Vintage Books, 1995.

Emerson, Ralph Waldo. "Boston Hymn." In *Emerson: Poems*. Edited by Peter Washington. New York: Alfred A. Knopf, 2004.

Fitzgerald, F. Scott. *The Beautiful and Damned*. Seattle, WA: AmazonClassics, 2017.

———. *The Great Gatsby*. New York: Scribner, 2004.

———. *This Side of Paradise*. New York: Scribner, 1998.

Forster, E. M. *Howard's End*. New York: Vintage Books, 1921.

———. *The Longest Journey*. London: Penguin Books, 2006.

———. *A Room with a View*. New York: Barnes & Noble Books, 1993.

———. *Where Angels Fear to Tread*. New York: Vintage Books, 1992.

Frost, Robert. "After Apple-Picking." In *Frost: Poems*. Edited by John Hollander. New York: Alfred A. Knopf, 1997.

Gaines, Ernest. *A Lesson before Dying*. New York: Vintage Books, 1993.

Gaskell, Elizabeth. *Mary Barton*. Peterborough, ON: Broadview Press, 2000.

———. *North and South*. London: Penguin Books, 1996.

Gonzalez, Manuel. "Escape From the Mall." In *The Miniature Wife and Other Stories*. New York: Riverhead Books, 2013.

Greene, Graham. *Brighton Rock*. London: Penguin Books, 2004.

———. *The Heart of the Matter*. London: Penguin Books, 2004.

———. *The Power and the Glory*. New York: Viking Press, 1940.

H.D. "Sheltered Garden." In *H.D.: Selected Poems*. Edited by Louis Martz. New York: New Directions, 1988.

Hardy, Thomas. "The Darkling Thrush." In *Thomas Hardy: The Complete Poems*. Edited by James Gibson. New York: Palgrave, 2001.

Hawthorne, Nathaniel. *The Scarlet Letter*. New York: Holt, Rinehart & Winston, 1964.

Hemingway, Ernest. *A Farewell to Arms*. New York: Scribner, 2014.

———. *For Whom the Bell Tolls*. New York: Charles Scribner's Sons, 1940.

———. *The Sun Also Rises*. New York: Scribner, 2006.

Herbert, George. *The English Poems of George Herbert*. Edited by Helen Wilcox. Cambridge: Cambridge University Press, 2007.

Hopkins, Gerard Manley. *Gerard Manley Hopkins: The Major Works*. Edited by Catherine Phillips. Oxford: Oxford University Press, 2009.

Hopkins, Pauline. *Winona: A Tale of Negro Life in the South and Southwest*. Gloucester, UK: Dodo Press, 2008.

Hosseini, Khaled. *The Kite Runner*. New York: Riverhead Books, 2013.

Hughes, Langston. *The Collected Poems of Langston Hughes*. Edited by Arnold Rampersad and David Roessel. New York: Vintage Books, 1995.

Hugo, Victor. *The Last Day of a Condemned Man*. Translated by Arabella Ward. Mineola, NY: Dover Publications, 2009.

———. *Les Misérables*. Translated by Lee Fahnestock and Norman MacAfee. New York: Signet, 2013.

Hurston, Zora Neale. *Their Eyes Were Watching God*. New York: HarperCollins, 2000.

James, Henry. *The Ambassadors*. Oxford: Oxford University Press, 2009.

———. *The Europeans*. Oxford: Oxford University Press, 2009.

———. "The Middle Years." In *Henry James: Complete Stories, 1892–1898*. New York: Penguin Books, 1996.

———. *The Portrait of a Lady*. Oxford: Oxford University Press, 2009.

Johnson, Fenton. "A Dream." *Poetry* 14, no. 3 (1921): 128–29.

Johnson, James Weldon. *James Weldon Johnson: Complete Poems*. Edited by Sondra Kathryn Wilson. New York: Penguin Books, 2000.

Keats, John. *John Keats: The Complete Poems*. Edited by John Barnard. London: Penguin Books, 1988.

Lahiri, Jhumpa. *The Namesake*. New York: Mariner Books, 2004.

———. "When Mr. Pirzada Came to Dine." In *Interpreter of Maladies*. New York: Mariner Books, 1999.

Lamott, Anne. *Plan B: Further Thoughts on Faith*. New York: Riverhead Books, 2005.

———. *Traveling Mercies: Some Thoughts on Faith*. New York: Pantheon Books, 1999.

Lawrence, D. H. "Song of a Man Who Has Come Through." In *D. H. Lawrence: Complete Poems*. Edited by Vivian de Sola Pinto and Warren F. Roberts. New York: Penguin Books, 1994.

Lee, Harper. *To Kill a Mockingbird*. New York: HarperPerennial Modern Classics, 2002.

L'Engle, Madeleine. *Circle of Quiet*. New York: HarperCollins, 1972.

———. *The Irrational Season*. New York: HarperCollins, 1977.

———. *A Wind in the Door*. New York: Square Fish, 2007.

Leopold, Aldo. *A Sand County Almanac*. New York: Ballantine Books, 1970.

Lewis, C. S. *The Lion, the Witch, and the Wardrobe*. New York: Collier Books, 1976.

———. *Reflections on the Psalms*. San Diego, CA: Harcourt, Brace, 1986.

Lorca, Federico García. "Ballad of the Little Square." In *Federico García Lorca: Selected Poems*. Translated by Martin Sorrell. Oxford: Oxford University Press, 2007.

Maclean, Norman. *A River Runs Through It and Other Stories*. Chicago: University of Chicago Press, 1976.

———. *Young Men and Fire*. Chicago: University of Chicago Press, 1993.

Manning, Brennan. *The Ragamuffin Gospel*. Sisters, OR: Multnomah Publishers, 2000.

Márquez, Gabriel García. *One Hundred Years of Solitude*. Translated by Gregory Rabassa. New York: HarperPerennial, 2006.

Martel, Yann. *Life of Pi*. Orlando, FL: Harcourt Books, 2001.

McCarthy, Cormac. *All the Pretty Horses*. New York: Vintage Books, 1992.

McKay, Claude. "Joy in the Woods." In *Complete Poems: Claude McKay*. Edited by William J. Maxwell. Chicago: University of Illinois Press, 2004.

———. "The City's Love." In *Harlem Shadows*. New York: Harcourt, Brace, 1922.

Melville, Herman. *Moby-Dick, or, The Whale*. New York: Penguin Books, 2009.

Merton, Thomas. *The Seven Storey Mountain*. New York: Harcourt, 1998.

Montgomery, Lucy Maud. *Anne of Green Gables*. New York: Penguin Books, 2017.

Morrison, Toni. *Beloved*. New York: Vintage Books, 2004.

Murakami, Haruki. *Kafka on the Shore*. Translated by Philip Gabriel. New York: Alfred A. Knopf, 2005.

Norris, Kathleen. *Dakota: A Spiritual Geography*. New York: Mariner Books, 2001.

Nouwen, Henri. *Life of the Beloved*. New York: Crossroad, 2002.

———. *The Return of the Prodigal Son*. New York: Doubleday, 1992.

Novalis. *The Novices of Sais*. Translated by Ralph Manheim. New York: Curt Valentin, 1949.

O'Connor, Flannery. *A Good Man Is Hard to Find and Other Stories*. New York: Houghton Mifflin Harcourt, 1976.

Oliver, Mary. "The Summer Day." In *House of Light*. Boston: Beacon Press, 1990.

Pamuk, Orhan. *My Name Is Red*. Translated by Erdağ M. Göknar. New York: Vintage Books, 2002.

Pascal, Blaise. *Pensées*. Translated by W. F. Trotter. New York: Random House, 1941.

Pasternak, Boris. *Doctor Zhivago*. Translated by Max Hayward and Manya Harari. New York: Pantheon Books, 1991.

Percy, Walker. *Love in the Ruins*. New York: Picador, 1999.

———. *The Moviegoer*. New York: Vintage Books, 1998.

Proust, Marcel. *Swann's Way*. Translated by C. K. Scott Moncrieff. New York: Barnes & Noble Books, 2005.

Rilke, Rainer Maria. "A Walk." In *Selected Poems of Rainer Maria Rilke*. Translated by Robert Bly. New York: HarperPerennial, 1981.

Robinson, Marilynne. *Gilead*. New York: Picador, 2004.

———. "Imagination and Community." In *When I Was a Child I Read Books*. New York: Picador, 2013.

———. "Wondrous Love." In *When I Was a Child I Read Books*. New York: Picador, 2013.

Rossetti, Christina. *Christina Rossetti: The Complete Poems*. London: Penguin Books, 2001.

Rowling, J. K. *Harry Potter and the Deathly Hallows*. New York: Scholastic, 2007.

———. *Harry Potter and the Goblet of Fire*. New York: Scholastic, 2002.

———. *Harry Potter and the Half-Blood Prince*. New York: Scholastic, 2006.

———. *Harry Potter and the Prisoner of Azkaban*. New York: Scholastic, 1999.

———. *Harry Potter and the Sorcerer's Stone*. New York: Scholastic, 1998.

Roy, Arundhati. *The God of Small Things*. New York: HarperPerennial, 1998.

Ruskin, John. *Modern Painters*. London: Forgotten Books, 2018.

———. *The Stones of Venice*. Cambridge, MA: Da Capo, 2003.

Saint-Exupéry, Antoine de. *The Little Prince*. Translated by Richard Howard. New York: Mariner Books, 2000.

Salinger, J. D. *The Catcher in the Rye*. Boston: Back Bay Books, 2001.

Sayers, Dorothy L. *Gaudy Night*. New York: Bourbon Street Books, 2012.

———. "The Triumph of Easter." In *The Greatest Drama Ever Staged*. London: Hodder & Stoughton, 1938.

Sebald, W. G. *Austerlitz*. Translated by Anthea Bell. New York: Modern Library, 2011.

———. *The Rings of Saturn*. Translated by Michael Hulse. New York: New Directions Books, 1999.

Shakespeare, William. *Hamlet*. New York: Blaisdell, 1939.

———. *King Lear*. New York: Ginn, 1940.

———. "Let me not to the marriage of true minds" (Sonnet 116). In *The Oxford Shakespeare: The Complete Sonnets and Poems*. Edited by Colin Burrow. Oxford: Oxford University Press, 2002.

———. *Macbeth*. New York: Simon & Schuster Paperbacks, 2013.

———. *Much Ado about Nothing*. New York: Simon & Schuster Paperbacks, 2018.

———. *Othello*. New York: Simon & Schuster Paperbacks, 2017.

———. *Romeo and Juliet*. New York: Washington Square Press, 1992.

Shelley, Mary. *The Last Man*. Oxford: Oxford University Press, 2008.

Silko, Leslie Marmon. *Ceremony*. New York: Penguin Books, 2006.

Smith, Betty. *A Tree Grows in Brooklyn*. New York: HarperPerennial, 2006.

Smith, Zadie. *On Beauty*. New York: Penguin Press, 2005.

Spiegelman, Art. *Maus I: A Survivor's Tale; My Father Bleeds History*. New York: Pantheon Books, 1986.

Steinbeck, John. *The Grapes of Wrath*. New York: Penguin Books, 2002.

Tan, Amy. *The Joy Luck Club*. New York: Penguin Books, 2006.

Tanizaki, Jun'ichirō. *In Praise of Shadows*. Translated by Thomas J. Harper and Edward G. Seidensticker. Sedgwick, ME: Leete's Island Books, 1977.

Taylor, Barbara Brown. *An Altar in the World: A Geography of Faith*. New York: HarperCollins, 2009.

Thoreau, Henry David. *Walden*. In *Walden and Other Writings by Henry David Thoreau*. New York: Modern Library, 1992.

Tolkien, J. R. R. *The Fellowship of the Ring*. New York: Houghton Mifflin Harcourt, 2004.

Tolstoy, Leo. *Anna Karenina*. Translated by Richard Pevear and Larissa Volokhonsky. New York: Penguin Books, 2002.

———. "What Men Live By." In *What Men Live By, and Other Tales*. Translated by Aylmer Maude and Louise Maude. Rockville, MD: Wildside Press, 2004.

Truth, Sojourner. *Narrative of Sojourner Truth*. New York: Penguin Books, 1998.

Twain, Mark. *The Adventures of Huckleberry Finn*. New York: W. W. Norton, 1998.

Walker, Alice. *The Color Purple*. Boston: Houghton Mifflin Harcourt, 1992.

Welty, Eudora. *The Eye of the Story: Selected Essays and Reviews*. New York: Vintage Books, 1990.

Wesley, Charles. "Morning Hymn." In *John and Charles Wesley: Selected Prayers, Hymns, Journal Notes, Sermons, Letters, and Treatises*. Edited by Frank Whaling. Mahwah, NJ: Paulist Press, 1981.

———. "My God! I know, I feel thee mine." In *Hymns and Sacred Poems*. London: Forgotten Books, 2017.

Wharton, Edith. *The Age of Innocence*. Oxford: Oxford University Press, 2006.

———. *The House of Mirth*. Oxford: Oxford University Press, 1999.

Wheatley, Phillis. "On Virtue." In *Phillis Wheatley: Complete Writings*. Edited by Vincent Carretta. New York: Penguin Books, 2001.

Whitman, Walt. *Leaves of Grass*. Nashville: American Renaissance Books, 2009.

———. "When I Heard the Learn'd Astronomer." In *Walt Whitman: The Complete Poems*. Edited by Francis Murphy. New York: Penguin Books, 2004.

Whittier, John Greenleaf. *The Complete Poetical Works of John Greenleaf Whittier*. London: Forgotten Books, 2012.

Wilde, Oscar. *An Ideal Husband*. In *The Importance of Being Earnest and Other Plays*. Oxford: Oxford University Press, 2007.

———. *The Picture of Dorian Gray*. Oxford: Oxford University Press, 2008.

Index of Literary Sources

NOVELS/SHORT STORIES/PLAYS